FUSE

MIROLAND IMPRINT 28

**Canada Council   Conseil des Arts
for the Arts   du Canada**

ONTARIO ARTS COUNCIL
CONSEIL DES ARTS DE L'ONTARIO

an Ontario government agency
un organisme du gouvernement de l'Ontario

Canadä

Guernica Editions Inc. acknowledges the support of the Canada Council
for the Arts and the Ontario Arts Council. The Ontario Arts Council
is an agency of the Government of Ontario.

We acknowledge the financial support of the Government of Canada.

FUSE

Hollay Ghadery

MiroLand
publishers

MIROLAND (GUERNICA)
TORONTO • CHICAGO • BUFFALO • LANCASTER (U.K.)
2021

Connie McParland, series editor
Gary Clairman, editor
David Moratto, cover and interior design
Guernica Editions Inc.
287 Templemead Drive, Hamilton, ON L8W 2W4
2250 Military Road, Tonawanda, N.Y. 14150-6000 U.S.A.
www.guernicaeditions.com

Distributors:
Independent Publishers Group (IPG)
600 North Pulaski Road, Chicago IL 60624
University of Toronto Press Distribution,
5201 Dufferin Street, Toronto (ON), Canada M3H 5T8
Gazelle Book Services, White Cross Mills
High Town, Lancaster LA1 4XS U.K.

First edition.
Printed in Canada.

Legal Deposit—First Quarter
Library of Congress Catalog Card Number: 2020947888
Library and Archives Canada Cataloguing in Publication
Library and Archives Canada Cataloguing in Publication
Title: Fuse / Hollay Ghadery.
Names: Ghadery, Hollay, author.
Description: First edition.
Identifiers: Canadiana (print) 20200359894 | Canadiana (ebook) 20200359967
| ISBN 9781771835923 (softcover) | ISBN 9781771835930 (EPUB)
| ISBN 9781771835947 (Kindle)
Subjects: LCSH: Ghadery, Hollay. | LCSH: Racially mixed women—Race identity.
| LCSH: Racially mixed women—Mental health.
| LCSH: Women—Identity. | LCGFT: Essays.
Classification: LCC PS8613.H33 F87 2021 | DDC C814/.6—dc23

To my family.
Dooset daram.

If I had a god
I'd say we were holy and didn't know it,
but I see only what we make of ourselves on earth
how long it takes for us to love what we are.
　　—Bronwen Wallace, "What it Comes To Mean"

She knew what she knew, and it was not the last
time she was to experience those sudden spasms
of comprehension of simultaneous worlds.
　　—Adele Wiseman, *Crackpot.*

Contents

Foreword

I BEGAN THIS project with a clear idea: I was going to write about the documented prevalence of eating disorders and body image issues in biracial women. I would use my experiences as a half-Iranian, half-white woman of European descent to dive into the conflicts and uncertainties surrounding the biracial female body and identity.

And that, I thought, would be that.

As I began writing, it became obvious that I wouldn't be able to keep my project as contained as I had hoped. I couldn't write about the experience of being a biracial woman without also talking about the experience of being labelled. I was writing about race, body and identity, yes, but there was considerably more subtext. I was also writing about how living in a way that defies strict categorization puts one at odds with a world that often demands that people justify and position themselves and their choices.

Then there was the eating disorder. I couldn't write about eating disorders without tackling the underlying mental health issues. I couldn't talk about mental health without unpacking the role nurture and nature play in the development of psychological well-being. I would need to talk about my family, which I was hesitant to do, in detail. I feared misrepresenting them. I was terrified that, if I spoke of how we had failed each other, people would dismiss all the ways we have fought for one another too. I was afraid people wouldn't see how much I love them.

I also knew that if I talked about my mental health, I would need to talk about my substance abuse, my self-mutilation, self-hatred, and an anxiety disorder that had become so overpowering that it almost killed me. I mean, I almost killed myself. I mean both.

The ever-expanding scope of my project meant that I would need to admit things about myself that I didn't want to acknowledge, and the trajectories of these admissions would make it nearly impossible for me to maintain a linear narrative. Once I opened the door a crack to one truth, they all came tumbling in and they didn't come in a manner that immediately made sense either. I spent the last four years picking them up and picking them apart. Sometimes these truths wouldn't be separated. Something was holding them together. My task was to figure out what. I was going to have to rethink the structure of the book.

A conventional memoir storyline wasn't getting me anywhere because it demanded an omniscient wisdom and detachment that I felt undermined the recounting of my experience. It was essential that I convey this overwhelming feeling, because without its weight, it would be impossible for anyone else to understand my reality. To paraphrase a line from Robert Pirsig's *Zen and the Art of Motorcycle Maintenance*: Reality is the vision before intellectualization. This—the battered and inarticulate self—this was my experience of mental illness. This is what I wanted to expose.

I followed the underground currents of my experiences wherever they took me, even when they kept bringing me back to the same place—especially when they kept bringing me back to the same place. I prioritized the thematic connections over chronology until gradually the links between thoughts, feelings, and experiences began to reveal themselves. This book is a collection of these intersections. Some of them are more meditative, and others serve to illustrate the rawness of experience. I share them here for the same reasons I think that all stories are told: To teach. To learn. To bring us together.

Waiting for Wonder Woman

"**S**EE WHAT I mean? The only way in is around."

But Nuala doesn't see. She is hopping from foot to foot, as if the ground is on fire. She's hot. It is hot. The parking lot is a sprawl of swollen concrete and asphalt. We're going to a movie, and I've realized too late that I parked on the wrong side of the huge multiplex theatre. We have to walk to the other side of the building to get to the entrance.

Nuala tugs on my arm. "Can you carry me?"

"What's wrong with your legs?"

She lets her body melt forward. She pulls at the shoulders of her puffed sleeve pink taffeta dress.

"Mooommmmmmy …" What she wants to say is that her dress is stifling and itchy, which I told her it would be, but she insisted on wearing it. What she does say is: "This is taking so long."

Nuala is five and when you're little, there's little of your life that's yours to control; so much is decided for you. In the absence of pre-science, a great many things can feel like they're taking too long.

"We're almost there," I say. The greasy smack from the theatre's dumpsters hits us. She crinkles her nose, which emphasizes its pixie upturn. I offer my hand. "Hold?"

Nuala laces her fingers through mine and brings our hands to her eye level. She squints, her eyelashes like gold tinsel, throwing light.

"Your skin is darker than mine."

"Um hm."

"But not by much."

"No, not by much."

I know where this is going. She peers more closely at our intertwined fingers. We've had this conversation before, in different incarnations. Nuala wants proof she's mine.

"And I have long hair," she says, dropping our hands from in front of her face. "I have long hair like you."

"Yes, like me."

"But blonde." As she says this, she frowns.

"Yes, blonde," I confirm, trying to run my fingers through her hair but getting them snagged in knots. "It's beautiful."

"But long like yours?" She is asking for assurance because she's afraid.

"Long exactly like mine."

She's afraid she doesn't belong to me. This is what she has said. Everyone tells her she doesn't look anything like me, and it scares her. When I was Nuala's age, I didn't look much like my mother either. I've told Nuala this, but still, she worries.

My mom's appearance: grey-blue eyes, auburn hair, gap-toothed smile, soft, peach-fuzz skin, wide face. Mine: coarser, darker.

Much darker. I didn't look like my mom, but it didn't cause me distress.

"I look like Daddy," Nuala says. "Like you look like your Daddy."

Yes, I look more like my father: prominent Persian nose, oval face, wide smile, thick skin. More, but not the same. I'm lighter than my dad. My mother's British Isle background diluted my father's Iranian looks: My hazel eyes to his chestnut. My hair, the colour of molasses and kerosene to his, dark as coal. My deep olive skin to his Lut-desert tan.

Nuala starts swinging my arm as we walk, pulling it jerkily back and forth. It's partly out of play, and in part to remind me how uncomfortable she is in this heat. We round the building and are met with a five-story poster of Wonder Woman: a tower of gloss. Nuala looks up, shielding her eyes against the glare of the photo with her hand.

Our arms swing to a stop.

"There she is," she says, nodding her head toward the image.
I take a deep breath in.

⎯⎯⎯+ I grew into looking like my mother. At certain points in our lives, we've looked incredibly similar, but we've never looked the same at the same time. Still, if you had a picture of us both at an identical age, say, the age I am now—me at thirty-six and her at thirty-six—you'd notice something similar about the way we hold ourselves: the affected ease. Both of us have had a few kids, and are paying down mortgages and working part-time from home, my mom as a seamstress, and me as a freelance writer. In the photo of my mom, she's standing on a silk Persian rug, wearing a belted, shoulder-padded, mid-length, Alice-blue dress, black pumps, and chunky 24-karat gold jewellery my dad has brought back from business trips to Hong Kong. Her short hair has been freshly dyed a deep red, curled, and sprayed into a tight coif. She's smiling self-consciously; a smile that's toothy, but not open. It's 1987.

In the picture of me, I'm wearing cheap pearl knock-off earrings from Joe Fresh and a black cotton racer tank top. I'm sitting at a table in a restaurant, so you can't see that I'm wearing skinny jeans. But I am. They are blue and distressed. I'm probably wearing flip-flops too. My hair is long enough to extend beyond the periphery of the picture. It's not dyed, but is growing lighter with age. It's becoming streaked with white, not that you can notice that in this picture. You'd have to get close, and I'm probably not going to let you because I'm over-smiling with my famous "Guy Smiley grin". It means *get back*. It means I'm defending myself against the suspicion that this picture is going to make me look unintentionally stupid, so I'll make sure that I look stupid on purpose. Smile big. Say cheese.

Now take both of these pictures, and put them side-by-side. You'll see the same arched brows, high cheekbones and almond-shaped eyes. You'll see that one way or another, we're both holding back.

⎯⎯⎯+ Nuala is pulling at my arm again, trying to move me in the direction of the theatre entrance.
"Is Nana here already?" She asks this as we cross the final stretch

of concrete. I've forgotten to text my mother to let her know we're running late. PST, we call it: Persian Standard Time. I fish my phone out of my purse and realize that she has already texted three times. She's waiting at the box office.

Nuala and I see her once we're through the doors and our eyes have adjusted from the light outside. My mom waves, mouth set in a crisp line, showing her disapproval for me. Nuala bounces over to her, dress billowing up with each bound.

"Nana!" She squeals, collapsing around my mother's legs.

Smiles for Nuala.

"That," my mother explained, "is an Amazon. Amazons were a tribe of women warriors in Greek mythology."

I was nine years old, standing in the stairwell of my grandfather's cottage and staring at a painting of a woman with burnt-caramel skin. She was posed against a blood-red backdrop. The painting had been on the wall for as long as I'd been alive, but I only noticed it then. I don't know how or why these awakenings happen to us when they do, but suddenly, she was there: full, familiar, and foreign, and all at once. I was transfixed, rooted in an amber wedge afternoon, thick and sweet as my grandfather's jars of lilac honey.

This was where my mom found me on her way upstairs to get dry towels for my brothers. She had our popsicle beach towels folded over her arm, the ones we got by collecting popsicle sticks. We would save our sticks until we'd earned enough points to redeem them for prizes. My brothers were still swimming in the lake with my cousins. I could hear their shrieks of laughter through the open window at the top of the stairs along with the hum of bees and the crickets; the pleasant pulsing heat and the waves lapping against the side of my grandfather's old green boat house, which was beginning to slouch into the lake.

"One of her breasts is removed because this would make it easier for her to use her bow," my mom continued, pointing to the Amazon's chest, and then to her arm, which was pulled back, at full draw on her arrow. I unconsciously brought my hand to my chest and twisted my skin through my shirt. There was enough of it: skin and chicken cutlet fat. Enough to signal the beginning of that pudgy pubescent stage that many girls transition into, and some never come out of. Not really.

I twisted harder and my eyes widened. Still, I couldn't seem to open them enough to take the picture in: her black hair, a brass headband, a leather wrist cuff. She was all sinew, form and focus. She was bulk and beauty and fearlessness. The skirt of her short dress cupped her round buttocks, pulling tight over her wide hips, and one thick leg was positioned behind the other, taut, unmovable. I tried to imagine her pain, strength, and beauty, existing together like that.

"Do they still exist?" I looked up at my mother.

"The Amazons?" She raised an eyebrow.

I nodded.

"I'm not sure."

The hand that had been clutching my chest fell to my side. The other reached out to trace the Amazon's aquiline nose, her elbow. Sun from the window started to pick up refractions of light in the paint. Her skin seemed to prickle, the muscles in her draw arm tensed.

My mom stroked my hair. "I'm not sure they *ever* did exist."

———⤳ My first sighting of Hollywood's latest Amazon Wonder Woman was on a can of Diet Dr. Pepper. My husband Matthew and I were out for lunch, and I'd pointed to the can. My parents had the kids for a sleepover, and we used the opportunity to do some child-free grocery shopping and grab a meal.

"Who the hell is this supposed to be?" I held up my drink and pointed to the slim woman clutching a sword and shield.

Matthew glanced up from unwrapping his BBQ steak pita. Instead of answering, he offered information.

"Did you know that her costume was so tight she couldn't breathe, but she didn't want to say anything, so she just, you know, suffered until someone in costume noticed?"

"Where did you hear that?" It was unlike Matthew to know anything about celebrity culture.

"It was a news story that someone on Facebook shared. I thought of you."

"Is it true?"

"I guess so." He scratched his beard, leaving BBQ sauce in his whiskers. "It sounded like it might be true, but I didn't click through to read the whole article." He bit into his pita and more BBQ sauce squirted out of the end onto the table. He wiped it up with a napkin and tossed it in a can on the other side of the table.

"That's recycling," I said.

"Shit."

While he was retrieving the napkin, I Googled the interview on my phone. *Wonder Woman costume too tight for actor.*

It was true enough.

"'I COULDN'T BREATHE': GAL GADOT ADMITS HER WONDER WOMAN COSTUME WAS TOO TIGHT ... UNTIL SHE STARTED REGULAR WORKOUT ROUTINE."

I searched for more pictures of this Hollywood Wonder Woman and had to blink the images in slowly, one at a time. She was nothing like the Amazon in my grandfather's stairwell. Nothing like the Wonder Woman I'd subsequently sought out in my brothers' comic books. As a comic book character, depending on who drew her, her appearance changed, but from what I saw, her fuller-bodied freedom was a constant.

As a preteen, this Wonder Woman offered me the possibility of seeing another sort of beauty: someone else when I looked in the mirror. Not the chubby, awkward, mixed-race girl whom boys in her all-white class teased about the dark hair on her upper lip. Not the girl who used to try to hide in the bathroom on track and field day because she was ashamed of the thickness of her body. Wonder Woman's body embodied hope.

Matthew sat back down and wiped his hands on his thighs before picking up his pita again.

I was starting to feel an old familiar rage surfacing. When would girls and women who looked like me *ever* be enough? I didn't know it until Matthew grabbed my hands, but I was crying.

"Hey." Matt lowered my phone so I had to look at him.

"It's just ..." I yanked my sleeve over my hand and wiped at my face. "It's so stupid of me."

"It's not." He paused. "What is it?"

I looked around. The restaurant was empty. The refrigerator be-hind the counter shuddered. "It's just ... I'm just so fucking mad." I sputter-laughed and began crying in earnest. I held up my phone, shov-ing the screen in his face. "They could have done so much better than this. And this." I jabbed toward the can of soda. "They could have done so much more than this shit."

Matt shifted his eyes between the phone and the can, processing the pictures.

"What? Is it the commercialism, the woman, the aspartame, or ...?"

"The first two, I guess. Or all of them. I mean, they're connected, aren't they?" They chose a woman who looks like that because she's more appealing to everyone, and slap her on a mass produced, zero-calorie drink.

"Okay." He nodded slowly, one cheek full of pita. He swallowed hard. "Yes, they are."

Even though I hadn't seen the movie or a single preview, I'd heard enough about it to know it was being hailed as a major triumph for women: the first female superhero to get her first movie—and a female director to boot.

I took the napkin Matthew was offering and wiped my nose. "It's good." I said. "I mean, I know that in one way, it's good. But it's also not. Because it's always the same kind of woman; the same kind of body. It's always exactly the same shit." I spat the words, and even as I did, part of me didn't know why I was surprised by this anymore: the narrow idealization of female beauty, and my furious, impotent re-sponse to it. It has always been this way, as far back as I can remember.

Me at twelve: Pacing the family room and sobbing because I'm so fat. My adolescent pudge hanging over my jeans, my Persian nose al-ready so prominent that my brothers would call me Rhino, and the only place my squat little legs seemed to be able to carry me to was the fridge. I was crying because I'd just read another *Seventeen* magazine. It had praised the same long, lithe girls who looked nothing like me. They were narrow-hipped, fair-skinned, button-nosed. What was I compared to them? Nothing.

"There's nothing to cry about," my mother had said. "Some people just have good genes."

That made me cry harder. If they had good genes, that meant mine weren't, and I was doomed. I cried because I was hungry but was afraid to eat. As I got older, this anxiety swelled into a pendulum swing of eating disorders: anorexia and bulimia, bulimia and anorexia. At that moment, though, all I knew was that I wasn't making myself clear, somehow, because my mom was trying to calm me with a can of Diet Coke and a bag of Smart Pop and I was swatting them away.

And I'm still trying to explain myself, even now.

"It's the same shit," I told Matthew, "but if you try to point this out to people, they say: 'Baby steps, baby steps. The movie is the first, and the rest will come.' The proverbial fucking pat on the head of the hysterical woman."

I wiped my nose aggressively with the thin napkin, and it fell apart in my hands.

"I mean, are you fucking kidding me? We are way past baby steps. Girls are *dying*."

Matt handed me another napkin.

"Girls are dying, and the people who made this movie could have done something really great. They could have made a difference in some little girl's fucking life, a child who needs to see something other than another rail-thin, big-breasted beauty ponce about. They could have given someone different, something different, something beautiful and life-changing, and instead they give us ... this ... this ..."

"Yes, I know." Matt smiled: a small, sad consolation.

———— Nuala, my mom and I settle into our seats. This movie was Nuala's idea. I didn't want to go, but I promised her that, if she did well in school all year, I'd take her out of classes for a day and we'd do whatever she wanted. This reward system was really designed for my eldest child, Joseph, who was seven years old and showing no interest in learning anything that didn't have to do with animals, but I had to be fair. No double standards. So, Nuala, who never needed motivation to learn anything, had quickly and easily earned her day off. And she wanted to see Wonder Woman.

The night before the movie, while feeding Roo, our toddler, Matt gently tried to ask if I was going to be all right to take Nuala to the movie. He remembered our lunch.

"Jesus, Matthew," I snapped. "I'll be *fine*."

Joe had a school friend over, and they were talking over the too-loud TV in the family room. I recognized the drum-based, grunting music as being from a commercial—Nike or something. Guys doing intense workouts—flipping over tires, one-hand chin-ups, sweating torrents over and through ripped traps and lats.

"Guys." Matt raised his voice over the noise. "Turn it down!"

They did, and we heard Joseph explaining something to his friend. "Those guys on TV," Joe was saying, "they have nothing on my mom. You should see her work out, jumping all over. She lifts bigger weights than my dad even. She's tough. She'd kill anyone who tried to hurt me."

Matt looked at me, lifting one eyebrow in mock disapproval. I grinned and wiped peanut butter off Roo's cheek with my thumb.

"For real," Joe went on. "I know she only seems like a normal person, but my mom is a like an ant or a beetle. Way stronger than she looks."

Matthew put his hand on my arm.

I'll be fine, I mouth.

───⬦ By the first battle scene, I've started to sob. Nuala, too transfixed to notice, sits with her knees hugged up to her chest, her mouth open and glacier-cool eyes swimming reflections from the screen.

When I called my mom a few days earlier to invite her to join us for Wonder Woman, I told her I had mixed feelings. I told her this because I knew I wasn't going to be able to hold my tongue about my guttural reaction to the movie. My mother, I knew, might sympathize with my frustration about being left out of mainstream ideas of beauty and sex appeal. Still, at some point, likely before I was born, it seemed that she'd accepted the terms of the social contract, along with its mores and values. I had not. I knew we'd argue and I wanted to talk to her ahead of time to get the any disagreements out of the way.

"I'm not judging the actor's ability to act," I told her. "But the casting choice?" I was standing in the living room, cradling the phone between my shoulder and ear and trying to sort innumerable pairs of kids' socks. "I mean, you wouldn't cast Dwayne Johnson as a principal dancer in a movie about a ballet company. He and Gal both have great bodies, and I'm not saying that just because Gal is thin that she can't also be strong, or that because Dwayne is jacked doesn't mean he can't be agile as fuck. But they aren't ideal for the roles, and finding that ideal is what casting is about. There are other beautiful bodies that would have been better."

"But she's a goddess, too, remember," my mom had said. "Maybe she was just blessed with those good genes, so she looks less like an Amazon."

Good genes.

My mom still used the phrase on occasion, and in such a way that it never seemed to apply to me.

"*Mom*, even classic goddesses weren't portrayed like that." Aphrodite, Goddess of Love, was depicted as plump. Athena, Goddess of the Hunt, was portrayed built like a powerhouse.

I know my mom knows this, since she'd given me her books from university on classical literature and mythology. From these books and my continued reading, I learned that scholars and historians are still arguing about whether Amazons, in the strictest sense, did in fact exist. They debate whether or not—even in pure mythology—they would have cut off their breast for the sake of shooting accuracy. The general consensus is probably not. No ancient Greek art even depicts such a thing. These warriors wouldn't have needed to, since the draw arm is held higher than chest level anyway.

One thing is certain: actual warrior women have existed throughout history. Graves in Eurasia have been excavated and found to hold war-ravaged female skeletons buried alongside spears, battle axes, horses, quivers, and arrows. It's unlikely that any of these women worried about dropping weight to fit into their robes.

"I like women *theecker*," my dad chirped in. I'd tried calling my mom on my dad's cell phone when she hadn't answered hers. They were in the car, and I'd been put on speaker. "Theeeeecker," he repeated, drawing out the word in his syrupy accent. I could picture him goading my mom, elbowing her side. *Theecker.* He meant thicker. Chunkier. "They need a good dowry." He meant ass.

"So what?" My mom ignored my dad. "So what if the choice is just about selling movies?"

"Because, mom ..." I threw the socks I'd just paired across the room and let my free arm flail wildly. I sputtered. "Because girls are *dying*."

Years ago, when I was still struggling to start my eating disorder recovery, my doctor had told me that anorexia is the most lethal mental disorder, with four times the death risk of severe depression and twice the death risk of schizophrenia. He'd explained that the death rates of people with bulimia and "eating disorder not otherwise specified"—a term used to define individuals like me who exhibit a mix of atypical anorexia and bulimia—are also higher than many other mental illnesses. And despite all the baby-stepping, the number of people who are suffering from eating disorders is still on the rise worldwide.

"Let's end this discussion," my mom said. "I'll see you in a few days."

Just before she hung up, I heard my dad repeating: "*Theeeeeecker.*"

———• I'm crying in the theatre and it's not just because I'm angry. I'm crying because the actor does do a brilliant job, and the movie is good, and because it could have been so much better—could have meant so much more.

I shove a handful of Nuala's popcorn in my mouth. Superheroes are supposed to celebrate the triumphs of the underdog—the mis- and under-represented—and this Wonder Woman only does this in part. She's a woman, yes, but there's no real representation with this casting choice. We need to be seeing other bodies. Hearing other voices.

When the movie is over, Nuala and I say goodbye to my mom at the theatre entrance. I don't ask her what she thought about the movie, and she doesn't ask me because she already knows. Nuala and I make our way back to the car—me walking, and Nuala jumping, kicking, punching and whirling until she's a pink, taffeta flurry. The afternoon has cooled into evening.

I do ask Nuala what she thinks, though.

"I think she was awesome!" Nuala stops kicking to catch her breath. She pulls a strand of hair out of her mouth. "And she's okay, right?"

"Okay?"

Nuala grabs one of my hands and starts walking quickly around me in a tight circle, turning me with her.

"Wonder Woman seemed sad at the end, but she's okay, right?" Nuala is running now, and we're spinning. The tin-sheet sky flexes orange, red.

"Yeah, she's okay." I grab Nuala's other hand and spin faster until both her feet are off the ground. We're laughing, churning wind: creating a whiplashed orbit.

But she needs to be better.

Fuse

G IRLS ARE DYING, but it doesn't happen all at once.

The therapist searched my file. "Which one of your parents is Iranian?" She was pulling out my intake questionnaire. The form had taken me longer to complete than our session would last. I had registered through the outpatient program at the hospital, and after three months of waiting, I received a phone call letting me know I had an appointment scheduled for the following week.

"It's just that women who are biracial are prone to eating disorders," she explained. I nodded. I didn't ask why. I hadn't cared, but when she told me this, I jerked my spine straight, grinning and shrugging loosely and dumbly as a marionette.

This happened 14 years ago. I was twenty-four, and it was the first time I'd been to a therapist. I was only there because my boyfriend wanted me to talk to someone, and I would have done anything for him.

"And people with eating disorders are more likely to suffer from co-occurring diseases like depression, anxiety, and substance abuse," she continued, flipping through my paperwork. "And OCD. I see you've been diagnosed."

My eyes darted back to her. I'd been staring at the scuffed baseboards in her office, which I was pretty sure was, or had been, a storage closet. I was hungover, trying to piece together my surroundings. It gave me a small measure of comfort to be able to order my world there, since I couldn't remember how I'd gotten home the night before. I know there'd been live music in a dive bar. There were many vodkas and diet cokes. I remember giving a hair-tie to a girl who'd been throwing up in the bathroom. She offered me a slurred thanks and said that she usually doesn't drink that much. I told her that I usually drink 'til I'm hot. Haha. We both thought I was pretty funny.

Focus, I reminded myself, shuffling my feet under my chair. My jeans were digging into my hips. It was 2005, and low-waisted bottoms were still a trend, to the despair of anyone with a body mass index above 23.

Focus, I told myself again. I repeated the word over and over until the swarm in my head condensed into a dull throb, and until I could clear a space to take something in.

The office had brown stains spread across white dropped ceiling, boxes crammed into corners. One was holding a bouquet of fluorescent lights. Another, a tangle of extension cords.

The therapist was still talking.

"You were diagnosed with OCD," she repeated.

The system that gives names.

"When you were thirteen."

That gives me Brillo pad brains.

"The co-morbidity of these diseases is well documented," she continued when I didn't answer. I was not sure I had even blinked. My eyes felt dry; my skin, dry; my cracked tongue, impossible.

"They're connected." She brought her palms together, interlacing her fingers. "There's the need to compulsively control your world. The impulse derives from anxiety, which is why eating disorders and OCD are classified as anxiety disorders. Since this impulse is exhausting, people often resort to substance abuse—drugs, alcohol, and so on— to escape their anxieties. Then, there's the aftermath: guilt, remorse, and the return of the obsessive need to control everything. The cycle starts again."

Rebuild. Restrict. Release. Repeat. Got it. *Drink 'til I'm hot.*

The stains on the ceiling bulged oppressively overhead. I squinted, trying to erase them with my mind.

"In biracial people, this impulse often stems from tensions in the way they see and understand themselves. The technical term is biracial identity disorder. This is what happens when a person experiences no fixed identity. Each person will deal with it in a slightly different way. They may identify with one race, the other, both, or neither. Or they may identify in all of these ways—differently at various points in their lives. This lack of a solid sense of self can inform the development of those other disorders."

She looked back at the questionnaire, and bounced the tip of her pen off one of my answers. "And along with the OCD, you were diagnosed with depression. All in your early teens."

In addition to the questionnaire, I saw that she had medical records from my doctor. I recognized his classic near-indecipherable scrawl. My tongue loosened from the bottom of my mouth. I swallowed.

"Yes," I said.

My mom had taken me to see our family doctor because of my fixation on cleaning and tidiness: my frantic stab at order in the chaos. I'd become undone if things in my home were messy or out of order; I would cry, scream, and hyperventilate. I would not be calmed until everything was put back together in its place, and even then, the release of tension was slow, like air leaving a tire through a pinhole.

I remember the doctor saying something about an anxiety disorder, and by the time I was sixteen, after several more visits to the doctor, I was on the drug Effexor. I know I was sixteen because when I was told that the drug might make me gain weight, I felt terrified of taking it. I remember thinking, I can't be sixteen and fat, fatter than I already am. Girls my age were supposed to be lithe and nubile. I envisioned my body, expanding into an unrecognizable gelatinous blob—except for my nose, which hooked out like a prehistoric beak. I also remember thinking that if I took the medication, I'd need to keep it a secret from people at school, because I didn't want to be seen as different. Defective.

"And that." The therapist pointed her pen to my arm: "Self-mutilation. Another kind of release, another form of remorse and punishment."

I rubbed the thick bandaging wrapped around my forearm. The skin had already begun to heal unevenly. Eventually, I would have a puckered, jumpy scar with marked needle points on each side, right to left, from bold stitching that would itch and pull as the skin fused. But I didn't know that then. I just knew that I didn't want my boyfriend to leave me because I refused to get help.

"My dad," I said.

"Your dad?" She asked, looking from my arm to my face, raising a thinning grey eyebrow.

"My dad is the one who's Iranian."

"Okay." She made a note, and then nodded back to my arm. "Want to tell me about that?"

"He wanted to go to the beach," I said.

"Your father?"

"No, my boyfriend."

"Okay, and?"

"And it was too much. Because of this." I grabbed a handful of my stomach. "And this." I tapped myself on the temple.

It was too much, but I didn't want him to stop loving me for being too messed up, so we went. We drove along a country road and the way the paint hung off the barns kept me dead set on the grey vein of land. I hung off his words, scanning the lake—its wide wet eye, an open wound on my right.

"You've gotta lighten up," he'd said.

I'd worn a floppy hat, big sunglasses, capris, a t-shirt. The sight of my thighs squashed against the seat made me want to gag.

"That's the point," I told him, gesturing around my body, to the rumpled free-fall of my flesh. "That's exactly what I've been trying to do."

That day, he swam and ate, and got on with the other day-trippers. I waited on that beach, watching his head bob. I thought that I could wait. I could be beach-nailed as long as he pleased. I thought, okay, give me sea-shelled kisses, sun and suede-soft skin, ink-stained khaki shorts on the shore, this coke-flat feeling, and I'll sit here and wait forever, or as long as he pleased, because of all things, I loved him best.

——— The cut came later that day. That night. My mind was moving too fast. I couldn't fall asleep, and he was sleeping so perfectly that I was furious with him for every perceived injustice his perfection carried. I'd woken him up. Or tried to. And when he wouldn't wake up, I'd yelled, and when he got upset, I cut my forearm with the biggest knife I could find.

"How did he react?" the therapist asked.

The blood made him move. He was up and we were at the hospital before I could think of what to say to the doctor who sewed up my arm.

"What did you tell the doctor?"

I told him the truth: that I did this to myself, that my boyfriend had nothing to do with it. I don't know if the doctor believed me. He remained tight-lipped through the procedure, except to say: "I could sew this up more neatly, but I need to be somewhere else."

Whether he meant he needed to be with other patients or just get far away from me, I didn't know, but either way, I couldn't blame him. I wanted to be far, far away from me too.

"And your boyfriend? Was he supportive?"

He'd wanted to know what I was going to do if I ever had a kid—what I planned to say about the scar. I told him that I'd say it's magic. It could be a story about a caterpillar who fell in love with a girl and wanted to stay with her, always. The caterpillar didn't want to turn into a butterfly and forget her, since it's so easy to change and forget. So he crawled up on her arm and fell into a deep sleep.

Because love is like that.

My boyfriend said that I should just tell the truth. Black is black. White is white.

———+ I said to the therapist: "He was as supportive as one could expect, having to deal with me and all."

"Deal with you? Explain that."

———+ A few days earlier, he'd come back from a business trip, bringing with him stale train air, some scotch, a batch of expense reports for dinners and hotels, and an admission pass to a botanical garden.

He had to leave again soon, so he was trying a pointed approach. No time to mess around. He wanted to know what was wrong. No, that wasn't it. He knew what was wrong. We'd known each other for a few years by then. He wanted to know if he could do anything to fix it. I didn't know. I never did. But on that day, I knew that I was feeling desperate, because I'd been refusing to eat. I was refusing to eat, still. I'd just lost my job bartending at a local pub because I was having trouble retaining orders.

I wasn't going to tell him this, though. Not yet. He warned me that working as a bartender could make me feel worse about myself, and it had. There was the alcohol-induced attention from guys, and the knowledge that people were looking at me. And seeing … what? I didn't know, exactly, but I assumed the worst, because Julia Roberts' character in *Pretty Woman* had it right: The bad stuff is easier to believe. And I believed every bad thing about myself that crossed my mind, which gave me one more reason to try to empty myself of feeling anything that would remind me that I was tied to my body. I'd finish work, and then I'd drink. I was always hungover, tired, and hungry.

I'd been fired, but my boyfriend didn't know this. What he noticed was that I'd been spending a lot of time in the bathroom after meals and had lost weight.

He'd offer me a plate of dates, an apple, almonds, and I'd shake my head. No.

———— I didn't tell the therapist how I never even tried to make it easier on him.

I didn't tell her how once, after I'd thrown up so hard that my abdominal muscles screamed in pain, he made me herbal tea and started talking to me about our first date.

He'd said: "You told me I that wouldn't want to get involved with you. Remember? And when I asked why you made that little cuckoo motion at the side of your head."

He dried his hands on a tea towel and tossed it in a lump on the counter. My stomach tightened even more. I didn't remember saying that.

"Yeah," I said. "I was pretty drunk."

"On our second date, I took you to an ice cream parlour, and you ate raspberry frozen yogurt. Your shirt was the same colour as the counter. Do you remember? The colour?"

I shook my head. "No." Although I did remember it: an elated pink. The colour was memorable because I usually wore a lot of black.

The mug of tea in my hands was so hot it burned my fingers, but I refused to put it down. Pain was familiar, steadying, and I was afraid of where my boyfriend was taking the conversation.

He sighed and leaned back against the counter, his long arms bowing out behind him. "You know," he said, "I went through your closet, looking for that top once. It wasn't there. I was tempted to ask where it was."

I'd thrown the shirt out years ago, but I didn't tell him this.

"Instead," he said, turning to the cupboard behind him and putting away the canister of tea, "I stopped hoping I'd see you wear it again."

I stared at the back of his head: a curly, honeyed oblivion. I didn't tell him that I threw out the shirt because it reminded me of that day. His face, I recalled, was a radiance of expectation and that shirt had been fitted and cropped, showing a trimmer stomach, a belly-button ring. It reminded me that things change so quickly—between us things changed—and I didn't want to remember anymore.

"You never know." He turned and took the mug out of my hand, putting it on the table and crouching down to look me in the eyes. "One day, you could look in a mirror and see someone else. Like the person I see."

———— "What I meant," I said to the therapist, "is that I'm a tough pill to swallow. I don't make it easy for people to love me."

The therapist put her pen and clipboard on her lap. She leaned forward, reaching an arm out as if she was going to touch me, but stopped short and rested her hand on her knee.

"I very much doubt that's true," she said.

I shuffled my feet under my chair and forced out a laugh. Waving my hand, I said: "It's amazing how little of this has to do with him."

———— It's all about a white eyelet bikini that I bought when I was fifteen. It was the 90s, the golden era of supermodels, and I'd seen

Cindy Crawford wear something similar. I'd loved the bikini and tried it on in my bedroom, again and again, for months before I mustered the courage to wear it in public. When I finally did, I was at the family cottage.

"Lovely," a relative said. "One day, that will look lovely on you."

I've spent my life waiting for that day to arrive.

But there was a bikini before that: red with white polka dots. My mother had bought it for me, and my body hadn't reached a maturity where my father objected to my wearing it. I was only three years old, but I can still remember sitting on the end of my grandfather's wooden dock in that bikini and feeling a rising desperation. I wanted to cover my stomach, which protruded over the bottoms, bared to uncles, cousins, and brothers. The sun prickled my skin; the fine hairs on the back of my neck and arms began to stand up. This discomfort with my body, it couldn't have been anything I'd been taught. Not then. I was too young still. I was at an age when most kids ran naked through sprinklers, unburdened by their bodies.

I told my therapist, "It's just the way I am. The way I was born."

What I meant was: It's no one's fault in particular.

It's a little of everything.

—— It's me, shortly after my boyfriend and I moved in together. I was seated at my dressing table wearing my favourite emerald-drop earrings, an exacto knife in my lap, and vomit in my hair. I didn't need a therapist to tell me that I'd become my sickness. I didn't have to look in the mirror to see the broken blood vessels, puffy eyes, blood running over my chest, down my stomach. My boyfriend was standing in the doorway, at a loss for words. I was glad. I didn't need words. I didn't want to hear: *You're sick. You're crazy.* Every definition was a narrowing of what was possible. Of what could and couldn't be—and it tormented me.

My boyfriend had gone out for the evening; it's a gathering with the guys, he'd said. No girls were going to be there. Shortly after he left, I received a call from one of his friends' girlfriends. *Your guy's here with the whole gang. Where are you?*

I started eating: a loaf of bread, jar of olives, seven bowls of cereal. I'd just finished downing a glass of milk when the phone rang again. I reminded myself that control starts with small acts, like not answering the phone—especially if I felt that I should. I reminded myself that solitude is a good way to kill urgency.

Another glass of milk and I was ready to burst. I ran to the bathroom and let it all flood out.

My boyfriend came home earlier than I expected.

"Baby," he said. "There really weren't supposed to be any girls there. It's not that I didn't want you with me."

It wasn't the first time he'd done something like this. I knew he often needed a break from me, and the binge, purge, binge, purge cycle that would build all day from the moment I woke up. It was an act fuelled by an impossible contradiction: the need to perfect my body and the need to escape it.

"Honey," he knelt down in front of me. "I'm sorry."

I didn't care. I repeated this to myself: *I don't care. I'm going to run away from here.*

He cupped my chin in his hand and brought my face level with his. I looked at the mirror on the closet door over his shoulder. The blood had dried darker on the glass. I couldn't read what I wrote anymore. *Bitch? Cunt? Whale?*

Probably.

"Honey, please."

I was going to run away from there with empty hands and arms wide open, buzzed and broken by each moment, and I didn't care.

He brought me a warm, damp cloth from the bathroom.

"Do you want the hairdryer?"

I'd told him of how the sound of the hairdryer comforted me. An enveloping hum from my childhood, when my dad would dry my hair after evening baths and I'd drift off, warm and contained.

My boyfriend handed me the hairdryer and continued to dab the blood off my chest. I flicked the dryer on and held it in my lap. Closed my eyes. I felt goose bumps, a hundred fingertips all over my body: a star dying in my stomach. He worked gently, cleaning a gash between

my breasts. I put a hand over his, held it there a minute. Maybe all I
wanted was to feel my whole wasted body against his.

———⊷ "It has nothing to do with him," I repeated to the therapist.
"But he still wants me. And that's enough, right?"

"Is it?"

———⊷ It was for a while. A few years later, he let me know that our
on-again-off-again relationship was permanently over by booking a
flight home for Christmas without telling me. I dropped him at the
airport. His calm, self-contained centre had me breathing from a hole
in my heart. He said he loved me. I let him in. He let me out. He let
me go.

It's the blinking light of his laugh. On. Off. On.

I drove back to our apartment. It was winter-dusk; the sky was a
sheet of muted blue. There was all this space that opened above, un-
folded below, and even the trees were stripped to their waists. And the
birds. They'd taken to sitting one by one on the telephone wires.

He left, and I was careful to think of him in increments: digestible
morsels. A wrist, thick blue veins, lips on that warm patch of skin behind an ear, the small of his back. That indent on his forehead where
my thumb fit perfectly. I was careful to remember him just like this: a
plate of dates, an apple, almonds.

A re-imagined slice of afternoon where, when I'd shaken my head
at the plate, he'd understood that I didn't mean: All this is your fault.
I'd meant: It's always the same. I'm hungry as hell, but I can't tell if it
is coming from my gut anymore.

At the time of the appointment with the therapist, my boyfriend
was all I had. He had been all I felt I had for years. I told her about
how my father had cut me off financially and emotionally when I had
refused to transfer to a university closer to home after one year away.
He'd driven three hours to my campus, and took back the car he'd
given me when I was sixteen. He didn't tell me he was coming. It
wasn't something he would have announced to my face, but my father
was the uncontested sovereign of our family: a godlike figure. As with

God, messages seldom came directly from my dad, but through someone else—someone receptive, or devoted, or too afraid to argue. It was my mom who told me. She said I should lock the keys in the vehicle. He had the spare set, and would be there later to pick up the car.

"He says you're treating your body like a human toilet," she informed me.

"What?" I told myself that I didn't know what that meant. But I knew. I'd grown up knowing, hearing my dad talk to his friends or family on the phone in Farsi. *Khar kos seh. Jendeh.* At first, I did not know what these words meant, only that they were meant to be spat out. Eventually, relatives visiting from Iran would tell me. They meant: *Your sister's a whore.* They meant: *Slut.* I learned that women are either prostitutes or angels. They can never be both, and certainly never both at once.

"He says he knows people there, and they see you. He says they've seen you with boys."

I'd been sitting in front of my computer, the cursor blinking where I'd left off writing an essay. "Of course I'm with boys," I'd argued. "I'm at a co-ed university. Not a convent."

"He has pictures."

I was chilled. I didn't want to hear more, didn't want to know. *Jendeh.*

I still don't know why my mother told me this. I can guess: She was fighting with my dad, and wanted me to be as upset with him as she was. Or she wanted me to be ashamed of myself and come home. Or she thought she was preparing me for an eventual head-to-head with him by simply telling me the truth. Whatever the case, there's no doubt my being away was making her life difficult—or more difficult than usual, because there had always been tension between my father and mother, as far back as I can remember.

The therapist nodded, scratching her knee. Since she was still holding her pen, she ended up leaving a scribble of ink on her grey dress pants. "That may have been the case. The anxieties and disorders you are experiencing are more likely to crop up in women whose racial and cultural lineage is drastically different: like Russian and Chinese. Or like yours, of Iranian and white European. If you were to take someone else, of Italian and Greek descent, for example, the differences in their rearing approaches would not be as significant, even though these races are technically different. They share many of the same cultural values. Of course, most of us have to do some negotiating with the outside world to fit into predetermined standards of beauty. However, biracial individuals, whose parents' backgrounds are also markedly different in terms of culture, are often forced to fight a battle within the home as well: between diverging preconceptions about desirability and decorum, and the fundamentally different meanings attached to them. It's a clash between cultures."

She noticed the mark on her pants and rubbed at it with her thumb half-heartedly before continuing. "And since women generally bear the brunt of aesthetic and moral expectations in any race or culture, biracial women are the ones most likely to suffer."

She flipped a wrist with a tight flourish, as if by offering this long-winded explanation, she was offering clarity. But it meant nothing to me then. My dad had cut me off, sure, but I'd wanted out. Take the car. Take the funding. I wanted to be free, so I buried what my mom told me along with everything else, not realizing that even dormant words have lives: They take root.

———— "I know my dad loves me," I told the therapist. "He always told me that I'm beautiful. Beautiful and smart."

Jeegaretō bokhoram. Khoshgeleham. I'll eat your liver, my beautiful.

She gave me a dial-tone stare. "It has very little to do with an absence of love," she said. "Often, there's too much of it."

I loved him too. All of my family—I loved them all. So even though my dad had cut me off, I visited home as much as I felt could be managed, and always without my boyfriend. It went without saying that he was not allowed in my parents' house. I had moved away, and I was in a space that my father could not condone. My boyfriend was part of it; this sinister, chasmic darkness. So I spent Easters, Thanksgivings, and Christmases eating and drinking and throwing up in the bathroom. I think everyone knew, but the only person who ever spoke of it was my mother.

"Your father knows," she'd said. It was an accusation and a plea.

My mother was desperate and I could tell she didn't want to talk anymore about it, so I hugged her and said okay. It's okay. I'll take care of it. Because I could tell she wanted to be far, far away from it.

I didn't blame her. I wanted to be far away from it too.

———→ Years later, I would meet Matthew and we would get married. We would have a child: a son, and the first boy to ever own my heart completely. He would be three days old and we would be at his first doctor's appointment. He would be wearing a yellow and white Winnie the Pooh onesie that I'd swear was smaller on him since the morning. I'd think, please slow down. Stop growing so fast. Stay little and with me always.

My father and I would still be distant, so my son would be five weeks old before my dad would agree to meet him, his first grandchild. But everything would change when he did. The world would expand a little. He'd want his grandson close, close to him, and all would be forgiven. We'd both forgive each other because we love him so, so much.

———→ Around this time, I worked up the nerve to ask my mom why she told me about the names my dad called me—about the things that he'd said. I didn't want to argue, but now as a mother myself, I had to know her reasons for relaying that information. I didn't understand; I couldn't imagine why I'd tell my child something hurtful that someone said about them. But I was also a new mother. I thought, maybe, there was a reason and I was missing it. My mother said that she couldn't remember telling me any of those things; she insisted that she hadn't. But yes, she conceded, my father had said stuff like that. When I asked my dad about calling me these things to my mother, he said there are some things that a parent should never repeat to their child. Your mother, he said, should have known better than to tell you.

———→ Years later, when my son asks me about my scar, I tell him the story I'd practiced. "It's magic. It's the story of a caterpillar who fell in love with a girl. He loved her so much that he didn't want to turn into a butterfly and forget her. He wanted to be with her always, so he crawled up on her arm and fell into a deep sleep. Eventually his body became imprinted on hers, leaving this mark on her arm."

I told my son this story because I wanted to protect him from my jagged limitations, but I also felt, from the moment I saw him, an urge to offer up some sort of explanation. The story I created was my first stab at coming clean. I'd learn, though, as I started telling him more stories—as I started the painful process of trying to make sense of myself and the world that made me—I'd start to understand that things would never get cleaner, just clearer. Black is black, and white is white, but love: He showed me love is every conceivable colour.

Monster

MATTHEW FOLLOWS ME into the bathroom and I begin to undress. I'm in faded sweatpants and a black, bleach-stained tank top: my usual work-at-home attire. Matthew puts the toilet lid down and sits, leaning forward so his elbows rest on his knees. He's waiting.

The bathtub is already full of hot water and the room might be oppressively warm if the window wasn't open a crack, letting in the gooseflesh March afternoon. I put my foot in the bath to test the temperature. Scalding. The way I like it. I unhook my bra and toss it to Matthew, who hangs it over the towel rack. The bath steam heightens the scent of lavender oil, which Matthew must have added to the water.

For this rare moment, it's just Matthew and me. The kids have snacked and settled since arriving home from school. Now Joe, Nuala, and Roo are downstairs, trying to build a blanket fort with Harvey, who has entered the terrible twos with gale-force intensity. Roo, who is now in senior kindergarten, has recently taken to over-mothering her anti-authoritarian toddler brother, and it usually doesn't end well.

"NOOOO!" Harvey's shriek carries through the vents, followed by the sound of something crashing to the floor.

Matthew sighs and puts his head in his hands. I slip fully into the water, immersing myself until it sloshes into my ears.

I peer at Matthew from above the waterline. The heels of his hands are over his eyes, and the weight of his head rests heavily on them. I need to start talking. I sink a little deeper in the tub, holding my breath and trying to find a place to start. I already told Matthew some of the story when he got home from work: An article I'd written for a major news broadcaster had been published a few days earlier. The essay was about parenting with OCD, and how difficult it can be to battle the frantic rage that's part and parcel of this mental illness. There's the rage that springs up when something stands in the way of completing a ritual, like my needing to wash the floor every morning before I leave the house. Sometimes, last-minute spills and crazy schedules make cleaning difficult, if not impossible. There's also the rage I feel at my being a slave to these compulsive behaviours. I want so badly to be free of them. I don't judge other people's messy, well-lived-in homes: I envy them.

"I read the comments by accident," I continue the story for Matthew now.

He lifts his head and blinks. The skin around his eyes is red and strained from the pressure of his hands.

"I read them, but I didn't mean to. I was just trying to find my bio and picture, since I remembered sending them, but didn't see them when I first read the article online. So I checked again and scrolled down, too far down I guess because I found my bio and a lot of shitty opinions about me."

Matthew's eyes are intent on me, but he's still silent. I focus on my wet knees rising above the water, amniotic slick. I'm trying not to rush him, so I sink lower, submerging my mouth. Matthew, I know, is trying to be thoughtful in his response. Born and raised in blue-collar, small-town Ontario to white parents in a white-washed part of the province, he remembers only two families of colour during his entire childhood, and his only real experience with mental illness was harmless encounters with the town drunk. His parents were loving and attentive, but not political. Until he met me, his exposure to marginalized people and mental health issues was limited.

I don't doubt that I've taught my husband a lot about feminism, mental health, and racial and identity politics, but the education process has been reciprocal.

Years ago, before I met Matthew, I would have said that the tendency in mainstream culture—and by that I mean white culture—to not engage with issues that concern marginalized communities boiled down to a steamrolling sense of entitlement, a disdain for difference, or, at best, a disinterest. This is true in some cases, but it is not the whole truth. It's not the only truth.

At the heart of this unwillingness to get involved is something commonly felt and primal: fear. Fear of change, which includes other types of fear: Fear of being displaced. Fear of being attacked. Fear of the other.

I'm half-white, half-Iranian. As a biracial woman, I feel myself either straddling lines or choosing sides. When people who are racially marginalized criticize white supremacy, they are, I often think, criticizing me. When people criticize the subversives and 'others', they seem to be criticizing me. From this vantage (and *dis*advantage) point, I can appreciate how the rhetoric about the margins and within the margins can be challenging.

When Matthew and I were first dating and we'd talk about these fraught issues, it would only take one comment that I considered ignorant of him, and I'd be jumping down his throat. He once told me to "just be reasonable" when I was having an implosive anxiety attack caused by my inability to zip up a dress I'd been able to wear a few months earlier. It nearly ended our relationship. He knew I had an eating disorder. At that point, I was binging and purging almost every day, which had caused most of the bloating and weight fluctuation.

Matthew had been trying to appeal to reason, but anxiety can leave one with little. We were in my bedroom and I told him to leave. He refused—not until I told him what he'd said wrong. I told him again to get out, assuming his request was a sanctimonious insistence on his innocence.

"No, seriously," he said, grabbing my hands. "Please. Just tell me what I said wrong so I'll never do it again."

I'd entered the relationship with Matthew expecting him, at some point, to let me down. He was refusing to.

Sometimes I still have to remind myself that not everyone will let me down if I just give them a chance.

Matthew knew I had an eating disorder, but he had no idea what it was like to have an eating disorder. He didn't really even know what having an eating disorder meant, aside from the clichéd and often myopic depictions of the disease on TV and in movies, where it's just as often ridiculed as understood.

"My ignorance is my failing," he said, persisting. "But I'm asking you to help me."

In a movie we watched recently, a young Miley Cyrus portrayed a private investigator posing undercover as a sorority girl. During one scene, she makes a light-hearted quip about how she knows bulimia is the sorority's thing, but couldn't they show some love to the kleptomaniacs too?

It was meant to be funny, which is part of the problem. People who suffer from eating disorders and other mental health issues aren't taken seriously.

Chill out. Relax. Be reasonable.

When you're done feeling beaten down by these comments, you feel mad. And that day in my room, standing in a half-zipped up dress and feeling like a poorly stuffed sausage, I was mad. Still, realizing that Matthew was being sincere—that he wanted me to explain, to teach him—encouraged me to try.

——— When I said that the language of the margins can be challenging, I didn't mention that it can also be hostile. As I watched Matthew earnestly fumble to understand the psychological nuances of eating disorders, and as I realized how incensed I was at his failure to immediately grasp what upset me, it occurred to me how inhospitable the space for discussion can be.

——— I'm someone who's not wholly one thing or the other, but who's a whole person. I'm a whole person without a leg to stand on. As someone existing in what is for others an undefined and often invisible space, I understood the pain and frustration caused by being invisible or incomprehensible.

I saw it every day. On social media. In comment threads.

It's common knowledge that compassion suffers most in forums where people don't have to speak with each other face-to-face.

———⟶ Compassion is what is needed to start making positive changes in the way we talk about issues like mental health, race, and identity. As Matthew and I have continued our conversations, I've learned to make space in our dialogue for growth. I no longer spit hellfire every time some instance of insensitivity crops up, because it will discourage Matthew—a straight, white man, one of the people who could truly benefit from being a part of the conversation. Not everyone is as open to learning as Matthew, I know this, but a caustic response stops growth and learning. Period.

"Okay," Matthew says slowly, sitting up a little straighter on the toilet seat, his weight causing the lid to pop in. "So people in the comment thread were being dicks."

"Yeah, basically," I say, playing with the tub's diverter valve with my toes.

"But Kitty, remember why you wrote that piece: to help other people feel less alone."

Kitty is Matthew's pet name for me, taken from the Disney movie *Monsters Inc.* Kitty is another name for the character Sully, a big blue beast who is hired by Monsters Inc. to frighten children as they lie in their beds at night and collect their screams; the screams are then used for energy in the land of the monsters. Kitty is a name bestowed by Boo, the sweet, mischievous toddler who sneaks into the monster world. The child's irresistible and irrepressible goodness teaches Sully to challenge preconceived notions about himself and others. When Boo looks at Sully, she doesn't see a monster. She sees a kitty.

"And," Matt says, "you did get a lot of positive response from it. More than the negative, right?"

I nod, resting my chin on my chest and spitting a fountain of water out of my mouth.

"Then fuck 'em."

"One person said that the platform was turning into TLC—only featuring freaks."

"Fuck 'em."

"Someone else said that I emotionally abuse my kids."

I start to sink further under the water. In one stride, Matthew is kneeling by the tub and pulling me up under my arm.

"Fuck 'em," he repeats. "Seriously, *fuck them*. They don't know you or your kids. Your kids love you more than anything or anyone on the planet, even more than me."

"I'm a monster." I can't help my tears.

"Kitty ..."

"Crying in a bathtub is so redundant," I blubber, trying to laugh. I wipe my face with my pruny hand. "I'm pathetic."

"Remember what Joe told his class? When they were having a talk about family relationships and yelling at home?"

He said that his parents don't scream—at each other or at him and his siblings. This is true. We don't. But that's because it's not in Matthew's nature, and I can't start because I'm afraid I won't ever stop. I'm afraid that I'll unleash anger that I'll never be able to control.

"Why are you even with me?"

"Because you're everything but pathetic. You're not your diseases. You have this idea in your head that you are a terrible person because you have weaknesses, but you're wrong. You're strong. Even at your worst. You help me be stronger. You always push me to be better. You're funny, intelligent, caring, and beautiful. You're not some fucking project to me. I've always just seen you."

I shrug.

"Do you remember the night we ran into each other at that pub? That first time we really talked to each other?"

We'd seen each other at the gym but hadn't attempted much beyond polite greetings.

"Yeah."

"Do you remember the last thing you said to me when we finally left the bar at closing time?"

That was more than ten years ago. I have to think a second, but I then I remember and smirk. "I told you to make good life choices."

And I'd hugged him goodnight. I can still remember inhaling his citrusy bodywash, the brick wall of his chest against mine, and the way he hugged me back: carefully, but fully.

"Well," Matthew says, "I followed your advice."

I fiddle with my belly-button ring, but am smiling a little.

"Those people in comment threads don't know you," Matthew says. "And people who say stupid shit like that want to get to you. Don't let them. Do you think they could survive what you've survived and still keep going?"

I shake my head, mostly because I know it's what he wants me to do.

"Exactly, because if they could—if they had that in them—they wouldn't be emotionally dense enough to be making dumbass comments on a website."

I push myself back a little, so I'm sitting higher in the tub.

"I read other comments too," I admit. "Not on my article, but on others. People were especially horrible to women dealing with mental health issues. They said a lot of the same things they said to me."

"And what does that tell you?"

"They really are assholes."

Matthew laughs. He doesn't laugh often—not really laugh. He's self-conscious about his teeth, which are crooked. His parents couldn't afford braces for him when he was younger, and now he's just not interested in having them fixed. Still, he doesn't laugh openly much, but when he does, it's deep and shows his dimples.

All of our kids have dimples too. I picture their faces in my head; I can feel the soft give of their cheeks under my lips when I kiss them.

"It tells me that I can't let myself be bullied," I say slowly. "These are systemic abuses and biases against people with mental illness, and I shouldn't believe what they're saying. I shouldn't reply to their comments, because then I'd be giving them what they want: attention. And I shouldn't be reading these types of comments because it's not worth the upset. But I shouldn't shut up, either."

"Right!" Matthew slams the edge of the bathtub with his fist. "So what aren't you going to do?"

"Shut up," I say quietly. I still want to lick my wounds, but Matthew's revolution-style pep talk has me smiling in spite of myself.

"Louder!" Matt booms. "What aren't you going to do?"

"SHUT UP!" I shout so loudly my words reverberate off the tile walls of the bathroom, making me startle at the sound of my own voice.

"Momma!" I lean out of the tub and crane my neck to see Roo standing at the bathroom door, a torn open bag of jumbo marshmallows clutched in hand, at least one of the pilfered treats in each cheek, and a mass of burnt-sugar curls springing wildly from plastic Goodie butterfly barrettes.

"Don't swear!" she squeaks.

Matt and I look at each other, and he smiles again.

"Roo," Matt says, "Mommy will *never* shut up."

Completely Natural

I'D DYED MY hair black: like crows' wings in the sun. Strands kept falling in my face while I was unpacking, and every time they did, the colour surprised me. I wasn't used to it yet. It was part of my new look. I was moving away from home for the first time to attend university, and I'd wanted to look the part of a determined, strong, self-sufficient, and slightly mysterious girl. Woman. This, I'd decided, choosing the iridescent colour from a display of samples; this was where my life would begin.

It didn't feel that way, though. My mother helped me fold clothes and put them away, and I thought I was going to sob. Or throw up. Or both. I wanted to go home. But I'd worked so hard to get away.

I was in gifted classes until grade eight, and had done well in high school too, earning honour roll distinction, and one year, receiving the drama award. At that point, I was convinced I would be an actress. I abandoned this dream when I realized I couldn't keep people's eyes on me for any prolonged period of time. My anxieties flared up, and I was incapable of calming myself to remain in character. As I result, I tended to hyperbolize scenes, trying to act over the anxiety. More than this shortcoming, however, was the fact I enjoyed reading plays more than acting in them. It was the stories I really loved.

The only hiccup in my high school career happened when I failed grade 12 math. Most subjects came easily to me. Math had always been a struggle, and by grade 12, feeling frustrated and discouraged despite weekly tutoring and daily studying, I started to skip class. A friend, who was in the same class and also failing, would join me in jaunts to an ice cream shop a couple of towns away. We'd get frozen yogurt fruit smoothies and sip them on the way back, singing along with Big Wreck's *Blown Wide Open,* windows down, *all surrounded / by the things I thought I put away,* fields flying by. We'd return to school just in time to sprint to our next classes, cool strawberry and peach on our breath.

After receiving our failing grades, that same friend and I promised our parents we'd go to night school to make up the class. My guidance councillor had informed me that I needed a B+ average to get into the schools I wanted—schools that were far enough away to eliminate commuting as an option, but close enough to allow me to return home in a few hours. With this motivation, I took night school seriously. The teacher at night school had a different approach to the material, and my friend and I both passed, me with an A, and she with an A+. When I graduated grade 13 a year later, I did so with an offer of admission at my university of choice. My father could not contest its merit. It was a top school, but also a school that was a cool three-hour drive from home.

I was standing with my mom in my new dorm room, *Who Let the Dogs Out* blasting from a room down the hall, when my dad and younger brother decided they needed to go to Canadian Tire to buy a fan.

"You're going to die of heat up here," my dad had declared, looking around my cramped room, his mouth curled down in disgust.

The dorm window was large and overlooked one of the campus' tree-lined streets. The part of the window that opened, however, was only a little larger than a cookie sheet.

My younger brother was pacing. He was annoyed with me for breaking up the family. He told me this several times in the months before I left.

My father accepted I was going away to school, but he wasn't happy about it. He'd wanted me to be like my older brother, who was staying local and was on his campus that day seeing to last-minute course changes. My mother had supported me, and it had caused even more friction between her and my father. For the last few months, life at home had been tense.

My dad and younger brother returned. In addition to the fan, they had bottles of water and Fruitopia, which my dad stocked in my mini-fridge. His knees cracked as he squatted down. I kept my eyes on my dad as he emptied the bag of drinks. In that moment, I wanted to throw myself on his back the way I had as a child when he prayed; I wanted that reassuring up-and-down rocking, from earth to sky.

I wanted to trust his vision for my life—that what he said was best for me really was best. He thought I needed to be around my family. I'd need support while I completed my studies. He'd pay for everything. I wouldn't have to work. And when I finish my undergrad, he thought I should marry a doctor, lawyer, or engineer and go to law school. Becoming a lawyer myself, if not marrying one, was something I had been considering anyway. I could see the allure of such a career. From a distance, it looked safe and welcoming. But I also knew that the future my father dreamt up for me would have to start with my living at home.

Home. I only had to say the word and I'd feel like the air had been sucked out of the room. I pictured myself returning home with my family, walking into the large, bright front foyer; surveying the piles of laundry on the stairs, the blinding white tile that showed every speck of dirt, the coats and sweaters thrown over the railing. My mind travelled through every room, fixating on the clutter, dust, disorder.

No. I couldn't go home. I couldn't go home, and I couldn't tell my family that I was missing them already: that I was scared. I swallowed hard and fought the sense of swelling in my guts. What I wanted was to be able to tell them what I was feeling, and have them tell me it was normal to feel this way, and that I'd be fine. Better than fine. I'd be great.

I didn't want anyone to tell me that I could or should return. My mom might be tempted. It would make things easier between her and my dad. My dad would definitely tell me to come home, and then he'd have proof that he knew better: that I was as helpless and stupid and pig-headed as he thought.

As I suspected.

My dad stood up, straightening out his legs and groaning. I never

doubted that my father had genuine concern for me, but I also suspected that one reason he'd come with me to campus on my first day
was so he'd be able to say he was there, and had seen that it would go
wrong. That he knew from day one it would be a disaster.

A girl walked by my open dorm room door in a pair of fuzzy pink
Mod Cloth pants, and a cropped tube top. Her right shoulder blade
sprouted an elaborate floral tattoo. A slender belly chain lounged
around her waist.

My dad narrowed his eyes. I knew what he was thinking: *Low-class.*
He said: "It's too small."

He was talking about my room.

"It's a dorm, Dad, not a suite at the Ritz."

As we unpacked, he eyed the other residents and their families. All
girls. I'd wanted an all-girl dormitory. The idea of a co-ed dorm made
me squeamish. I had no desire to get up close and personal with the
showering and hygiene habits of my male classmates. I had two brothers. I cleaned their bathroom, and had to put up with their slovenliness.
No thanks. Not again. Granted, I didn't want to share bathrooms and
showers with my female classmates either, but if I was going to live on
campus, which was the most affordable option, I'd need to make con-
cessions. I did, however, manage to secure a single room. No roommate.
I knew that I'd need a break from the person I pretended to be when
other people were around. The black hair, the ripped jeans, the Beatles
t-shirt I was wearing—they weren't me. I didn't even particularly like
the Beatles. I didn't dislike them either, though, and I didn't know
anyone who did. That's why I figured the shirt was a safe pick. I wanted to be somewhat puzzling, but I didn't want to cause controversy: I
was leaving home to escape that.

My dad began fitting the fan into the window. Again, he said:
"You're going to boil in here."

My mom met my gaze and gave her head a quick, almost imper-
ceptible shake. I bit the insides of my cheeks.

I didn't know anyone in my residence. Unlike many of the other
girls who milled around the hallway, I had no high school friends there.
I could be anyone. I tried to take comfort in that.

"I picked you out as my competition," a dorm mate and eventual friend would say years later. "Because you were pretty, sure, but also because of your confidence. There you were, long black hair, a black t-shirt, looking tough as hell, and talking about your motorcycle, and how'd you'd bartended to be there. Then I walked by your room and saw the stuffed kitty cat on the bed."

Most of what I'd said that day was true. I did bartend to help pay for my first year. I worked at a shabby restaurant in a cathedral-quiet town where hardly any people visited. My dad hated that I worked there and told me frequently that I was disgracing the family, but by then I'd learned to tune him down, if not tune him out. My dad said a lot of things, but I never feared violence from him. My husband would eventually introduce me to a phrase—bullshit and bluster—that I think describes my father's sometimes explosive reactions. While my father fits many of the alpha-Iranian male stereotypes, it's important not to paint an entire people with the same brushstrokes. Just because my father is Middle-Eastern does not mean that his outrage or anger led to any kind of violence. And my dad's brothers, my Amoos, grew up in the same culture and were not as conservative as my father. They would often advise my father to lighten up and give me a little more freedom. Whether or not they afforded these freedoms to their own children, I don't know, since I'd only met my cousins a few times, but based on the advice they gave my dad, I assumed so. At that point in my life, I thought everyone was freer than me.

My bartending job had paid for some of my schooling, but it didn't pay for my entire year. My parents had started a scholarship fund for my first year of university when I was born, and my mother made sure I received that money. I didn't tell my dorm mates that, though. I went to a school where most of the students were financially fully supported by their parents, and I wanted to show that I was different. I wanted to show I was stronger.

And my motorcycle—I'd loved it. My father bought it for me so we could go on rides together. A Kawasaki Ninja 500. While we did go on long trips to the cottage or around the countryside, I was never permitted to use it alone, which made it one of the series of things in my life I couldn't love without restrictions. A motorcycle, a universal icon of freedom, became just another tool for controlling me. My dad sold it after my first year at university, realizing I hadn't bombed at living alone and was going to stick it out at my school of choice. His logic: If I wasn't going to be home to use it, why keep it? He took it away, and I was surprised to discover that I couldn't have cared less.

Nothing he tried denying me ended up mattering because, despite my anxieties that first day, I learned to love living alone. I'd never again have to take out my contacts before I entered my own house, just to blur the mess made by people I lived with. I could keep my dorm room tidy. When I moved out of residence, I knew that I could live alone in a bachelor apartment, or with a roommate who was as fastidious about cleaning as I was, if I could find one.

I didn't expect my problems to disappear. I knew I would still struggle with my OCD, my depression, my anxiety about my body, but I longed for a life in which I wouldn't have to fight a daily battle to control the order in my living space. I hoped my life would be easier. Living with an anxiety disorder was hard. Living with an anxiety disorder among people who refused to recognize it was unbearable. At home, my obsessive cleaning had become a joke: Want something clean? Leave it! Hollay will be home soon. My exhausting compulsions were something to laugh about, or something to be tolerated. These behaviours weren't seen for what they were: part of a greater problem. They arose out of an innate and unrelenting desire to keep my external world clean and uncluttered. It was a counterweight; a balm to my sparking, frantic, copper-wire-crazed mind.

I felt like the combination of external and internal chaos was killing me, while to most of the people in my family it seemed funny. I get it now. Here's the punch line: You can't laugh and breathe at the same time.

My cleaning wasn't a laughing matter when it caused fights. A couple years earlier, before I left with my mother on a summer trip to England, I'd cleaned the whole house, top to bottom. I'd made my dad and brothers promise to have it tidy when I got back. I'd made my mom promise to make sure my dad and brothers had it tidy when I got back. I remember her calling home on our last night away, quietly arguing with my father. I was pretending to be asleep.

"She's going to lose it if it's a mess."

Silence while my mom listened.

"I don't care. You promised her you'd make sure it was clean. So get the boys away from their video games and make them clean up."

It didn't sound hopeful. The whole flight back, I was bracing myself. I arrived home to a kitchen floor so sticky I lost a sock on it. Shirts were shoved between couch cushions. Dirty clothes were piled at the foot of the main staircase. The shoes at the front door were strewn about so I tripped over them when I came in. I wanted to cry. I did cry.

My mother took the backpack I was still clutching in my hand from me and told me to go upstairs and have a bath.

"When you come down," she said, rubbing my back and glaring at my dad, "it will be clean. I promise."

She got on the home intercom system. Static.

"Boys. Get downstairs *now*."

Boom.

I felt bad. I was causing trouble again. I felt sick, especially with myself. All I wanted to do, and the last thing I wanted to do, was to start scrubbing. I needed to do it, but I felt overwhelmed by the thought of doing it. I turned to go upstairs and passed my brothers coming down. They scowled at me. Let them be pissed.

I was angry too. They had weeks to turn the place into a shithole if they wanted, and I wouldn't be there to lose it on them. I'd just wanted them to clean up for me before I got home. And they couldn't even do that.

It's not like they hadn't known I had anxieties about cleaning, I told myself; they'd seen me sob, body knotted in frustration at the sight of jackets thrown over bannisters, food wrappers left on floors, tea-ring stains on the countertop. They had known what it did to me and they hadn't cared, so when they scowled at me, I scowled right back.

Now, twenty years later, I realize they may have known about my fixation on cleanliness, but didn't understand. It's an explanation that causes me pain. By just trying to rationalize their insensitive behaviour,

I justify it on some level. Where there is justification, there are excuses. I shouldn't spend my life making excuses for people who won't try to understand me, no matter how much I love them.

When I came down after my bath, the house was cleaner. The floor was sparkling. There were still pop cans and pizza boxes on the counter, but now they were stacked neatly in a corner. The dirty clothing had mostly disappeared. When I sat on the couch, I saw a balled-up sock under the love seat on the other side of the room. My father followed my gaze and sat down on the floor in front of it, tucking it into his back pocket before turning his attention to his cup of tea. He sipped loudly, straining the hot drink through a sugar cube in his teeth.

Slurp.

I could hear my mother in the laundry room, starting the dryer. My brothers were nowhere to be seen, but presumably they were back in their rooms playing video games.

My father continued slurping his tea, flicking through channels on the TV, and settling on *Ben Hur*. Through the open windows, the sulking scent of honeysuckle and sweet grass drifted in. The evening was on my skin, in my still-damp hair; it sent cool, comforting shivers down my neck. My body uncoiled. I stretched my legs, flexed my feet. Softly, somewhere in the distance, the stars were singing themselves to light.

I'm going to be okay. I told myself it was going to be okay for now, if I could just stay in this moment—if only everything would just stay as it was.

Of course, it never does. Life gets messy.

———• On that first day at university and for several days after that, I felt sad, but there was another, stronger emotion: relief.

The immensity of this feeling stemmed from the fact that my unhappiness at home had been about more than the dirty floors, piles of laundry, and cluttered counters. It was also about the fact that I was made to feel that there was something wrong with me. My mental struggles aside, the parts of me that I felt were untouched by illness, the parts that I felt were good and joyful—those too, apparently, were wrong. I missed curfew by an hour one night and came home to a

Magna Carta-style charter taped to my door. My father had written it. It outlined all the ways I was a disgrace to him, and how I would be punished.

I was a disrespectful daughter.

I was unappreciative of the things my father provided me with.

I continued to lie to him and go out with boys.

I had trashy friends.

I would no longer have access to a car.

My older brother would drive me directly to and from school.

I would not be allowed to go out with my friends, indefinitely.

The disappointment and punishments were nothing new to me. What was new in this instance—and the reason the occasion stands out in my mind—was the direct and formal communication from my father. He was obviously really angry. I can't remember now why I'd been late. I was just out with friends. It was unlikely that any of these friends were boys. I did have a few friends in high school who were boys, but these guys usually disappeared when they got new girlfriends. The high turnover of high school relationships meant that they acquired new girlfriends often. That night my friends and I were likely just driving around talking and listening to music. Our freedom was relative, but it was more freedom than any of us had experienced before, and it was intoxicating enough without having to resort to sex or drugs. When I said we were just going to hang out, my dad thought I was being intentionally vague. Yet truthfully, there was no better way to describe what we were doing. We were just relaxing: feeling ourselves in the world and the world in us. There was nothing mischievous about it.

But trying to explain this to my father wouldn't have helped. He once turned our car around while we were driving to an amusement park because a bunch of boys in a car beside ours were smiling, honking, and waving at me. I had done something to provoke it, he'd said. In truth, I hadn't even noticed them until my dad started lecturing me, but I'd ruined the day for everyone.

This is what it felt like all the time at home: I was ruining everything for everyone, just by being there. Just by being me.

After that first day on campus, when my father helped move me in, he only returned one time: on the day of my graduation. Once I'd received my degree and was walking back to my seat, he ran down the auditorium stairs to meet me. He was crying, laughing, and he enveloped me in a peppery cologne hug. Surprised, I scanned the audience for my mother, and found her smiling wide, eyes beaming blue starbursts. It was the first time I remembered making my parents happy at the same time, about the same thing. My mind was a feather—floating, ascending, and drifting away.

———→ Back in my dorm room, my father turned on the fan and started giving me detailed instructions on how to use it. The streets below were clogged with cars and vans unloading kids and boxes. I could hear shouts, laughter, honking.

I was half-listening to my father, but mostly thinking that he'd been spot on: I was dying of heat in there.

My mom and brother were gathering empty bags and boxes to take home. They were moving too fast and too slow. My dad was saying, "… and make sure the fan is pointing out to cool the room, not in …"

Breathe in, I told myself.

My dad's moustache went up and down, a prickly guillotine: "… close the window during the day to keep cool air trapped …"

Outside the ivy-choked building, the leaves on the trees caught sunlight like gold coins.

ENGLISH!

SOROOR IS A Persian name that means happiness. It's the name I gave my youngest daughter. Before that, it was the name of my father's sister, my *Ameh*—the Farsi term for an aunt on the father's side.

Soroor. The name is a prayer whispered under your breath. Like the feeling of happiness, the name trails after you, the final syllable lingering.

My Ameh Soroor was a soap bubble incarnation of her name. I say it and feel impossible lightness: Impossible because I didn't know her for very long; our time together spanned a few months at best. I met her for the first time when she and my father's other four siblings came to Ontario for a summer-long reunion at our house. Soroor emitted a radiant warmth—they all did—but especially her. Her warmth made her pliable. It was easy to fold her into my life, easy to want to fold myself into hers. Impossible because she has been dead almost ten years, and I still feel a surge of joy when I say her name. It's a joy that presses at the back of my heart.

My Ameh, like both of her sisters, didn't speak much English: a few words here and there. *Hello. Thank you. Bathroom.* After all of them married, they stayed in Iran. They had neither the cause nor the means to learn the language, even had they wanted to. My father's two brothers, my Amoos, had left Iran in their 20s, just like my father. It was a few years before the revolution started in 1978. They were seeking better lives. One moved to Austria and the other to Canada. My father stayed with this brother when he first came here. All of the brothers learned to speak English.

"It's the language of the future," my dad had said repeatedly when we were growing up. "Do not worry for learning Farsi."

But I wanted to learn. I'd ask him how to say certain words.

Ice cream. *Bastani*. Big. *Bozorg*. I love you. *Dooset daram*.

I'd listen to him on the phone with his friends and relatives, captivated by the lilts and tumbles of the language, its symphonic range of sound.

Having my dad's siblings visiting for the summer meant that I was able to pick up a little more Farsi. I'd repeat words and phrases they said, sending them into laughter.

"They aren't laughing at you," my dad said. "You just have an accent, and they think it's cute."

I never thought they were laughing at me, but if they had been, I wouldn't have minded. My brothers and I often teased my father about his pronunciation of English words. Strawberry was *eh-strawberry*. My dad told us there is no sound in the Persian alphabet quite like the initial serpent hiss of the English *s*, so he—like many native-born speakers of Farsi—have trouble saying words that begin with a soft s.

We'd make fun of my dad, and he'd say: "You try to learn to speak another language!"

I'd retort: "You won't teach us!"

When my dad's siblings arrived, I learned that they were also confounded by his reluctance to pass on Farsi. It turns out that the cousins I had, who didn't live in Iran, were at least speaking conversational Farsi. My dad remained dismissive, though. It didn't matter.

"Learn Chinese," he'd say. "Or Spanish. Or French. If you want to learn a second language, those are more useful." And then he'd add: "But there's no need for a second language. You should focus on learning English, and learning it well."

There's a compelling body of research that suggests that my father had a point, if only a minor one. Children who are raised in a bilingual environment have some disadvantages when it comes to linguistic range and recall. Bilingual children, on average, have less overall vocabulary in either one of their two languages than monolingual children have in their one. Bilingual children also tend to take a little more time to find appropriate words to express themselves. It makes sense. They have more words in two languages to choose from and need to think about which is best.

On the other hand, the same cognitive management that slows down their ability to choose the ideal word also enhances many of their executive functions. Working memory, cognitive flexibility, multi-tasking, inhibitory control, and conflict monitoring and resolution: These are all areas where bilinguals excel over monolinguals.

All these findings, however, were based on children speaking both languages regularly. In my home, that never would have happened. My mother didn't speak Farsi, had no apparent desire to learn Farsi, and didn't like it when everyone spoke Farsi around her. This was a well-known fact. When people who speak English are present, one should try to speak English to the best of one's abilities. That's what she said. She said it was rude to exclude people from conversation.

I could perhaps understand having this attitude when my Amoos were visiting on previous occasions: They spoke English, after all. But my Amehs didn't, and my Mom knew this. The majority ruled. That didn't make my mother happy about it though.

This exclusion, as my mother called it, never bothered me. I never felt it. Just because I didn't speak the same language as my father and his siblings with any degree of fluency did not make me feel that I was relegated to the outside. Even today, when I hear someone speaking Farsi in a restaurant, or store, or when I'm at the zoo with my kids, I light up; I feel the need to go over and hug them, pull them close and say: *Hey, you're here. I'm here. How amazing is this?*

There are around 60,000 Iranians in the Greater Toronto Area, so from a statistical standpoint, it's not that amazing. Still, when I hear the language—unexpected in my day-to-day life, I feel like some hungry, deprived part of my soul is being fed. Farsi is a language that may not be closer to the heart than any other, but it's closer to the gut; the plangent primordial ether of our being.

Perhaps I feel this connection, whereas my mom doesn't, because the language is part of my background. But I think there's more to it. My older brother and I, for instance, share the same background, and he could care less about learning Farsi. My love for Farsi goes beyond a biological connection. I love Farsi because being a part of this rare and beautiful language makes me feel rare and beautiful too.

So even though I didn't understand the nuances of what was being said around me when my Amehs and Amoos talked, I kept asking questions. I was learning enough to tell, roughly, what a conversation was about.

Dokhtar meant daughter. *Sigar* meant smoke, as in cigarette.

This conversation was about me. I had been caught smoking and was in deep, deep shit. *Ann.* The Farsi word for shit.

It was a Friday night in early summer, and usually, I would have been out with my friends. Instead I was being squished between my Ameh Soroor and the backseat window of my family's 8-seater SUV. Her perfume was so thick and sweet that I felt I could crush it against the roof of my mouth. My dad was driving. My mom, riding shot-gun. I was crammed in passenger seats with my Amehs and Amoos. My brothers followed in a separate car.

We were all on our way to a Persian restaurant for dinner, and even though I felt some of the indignant surliness of my age and situation, I didn't feel as unhappy as I might have.

I wasn't particularly unhappy at all.

My Ameh Soroor was laughing and I was laughing too, in spite of myself. I understood my dad had been ranting about my smoking, and my Ameh Soroor had told him to shut up about it. *Khafeh.* My other Amehs erupted into a chorus of cheers. *Khafe sho, Mojtaba! Pedarsag.*

Shut up, Mojtaba. Son of a dog.

My Ameh Soroor elbowed me playfully in the side and began clapping her hands along with the upbeat Persian pop music that had been playing quietly in the background. The rest of the siblings joined in. I saw my dad survey the scene in the review mirror. A smile escaped from under his heavy moustache and he reached over to turn up the music.

My mom sat impassively, staring ahead behind amber aviators. The tips of her ears were a painful red. She'd gotten a sunburn after spending the afternoon outside cutting five acres of lawn; it was her way of escaping the raucous presence of my aunts and uncles, and my father's showman-like efforts to control her behaviour in front of them. *Cook corned beef for them. Wear that necklace I got you in Singapore. Drive them to the grocery store or pharmacy or mall.* He wanted to make a good impression, show his siblings how far he'd come since their humble beginnings in Tehran. He'd purchased the SUV we were all riding in precisely for this visit. My mom had argued about the expense, and it had turned into a screaming match. I listened from the stairs and prayed for them both to shut up. Or for one of them to grow up enough to know when it's time to back off. It only ended when my dad left, slamming the front door behind him so hard the house shook.

They weren't arguing about anything now. Since that fight, they hadn't said much of anything to each other, not even about my smoking. I could tell my mom's burn was making her uncomfortable under her light summer shirt, but other than adjusting herself stiffly in her seat now and then, she sat cloaked in barely concealed distain.

What did bother me about my mom's feelings concerning Farsi was that I felt it put me in the middle of a fight I didn't want to be a part of. By wanting to learn a language that my mother believed alienated her, I feared that I would contribute to those feelings. That was not my intention. My mother never said she didn't want me to learn, or gave any sign that doing so would upset her, but I worried nevertheless. I saw how language could divide our house. We didn't need another Farsi speaker in the house to cause friction, either. My mother would even visibly tense up when my father spoke Farsi to someone on the phone. Who knew what he was saying?

It wasn't a concern borne entirely of paranoia. My father would make big decisions without consulting my mother or considering her opinion when she was consulted, like buying the SUV. Or, when it came to sending money to relatives in Iran or getting into business deals with them which she felt were ill-advised. She had valid reasons for worrying about what he was up to.

He could be overbearing.

I could understand why Farsi made my mom feel powerless. Her cool attitude toward my Amehs and Amoos, though—that embarrassed me. They may have reorganized the kitchen cupboards, or used fabric to make a headscarf that my mom had been saving for some other occasion, but if any liberties where taken in our home, that was my father's fault, not theirs. He'd given them permission to do these things. When my mother would complain, he told her this: It is my house, and they can do as they please.

It was her house too, legally and in every other sense, but that didn't matter to my father. He didn't see a division between where he ended and the people he loved began. They were an extension of himself and his rights.

The fabric for the headscarf, for instance: One of my Amehs wanted a replacement headscarf for when she returned to Iran. My dad had thrown the scarf she'd been wearing out the window on the way home from picking her up at the airport.

He'd said: "You're in Canada now. You don't need this."

Or maybe it was: "You're in Canada now. You need to act like it."

Either way, he'd taken the scarf off her head and sent it skyward on the 404, a brief buttercup flutter against blue before it disappeared.

"You're free here," he'd said.

This coming from the man who had no problem with my older brother dating, and even having his girlfriend sleep over, but who'd stayed overnight in a motel the first time one of my guy friends came to our house. The guy hadn't even come to see me. He'd come to pick up another friend of mine, the girl he was actually interested in.

But, *you're free here,* you know? Even though my dad had me right where he wanted: pinned in place, accounted for. And even though I was technically grounded for the next few weeks, and couldn't escape the helplessness of my situation, I thought of that scarf taking off over the highway, and I felt the freedom he had referred to. A least a little.

What I didn't think about then: that wearing or not wearing the scarf was my Ameh's choice. My father had no right to forbid it.

I looked behind me and could see my brothers following a few cars back. My older brother wanted to go out with friends later, and was going to leave right after dinner. He'd drop my younger brother off at home before heading out. My brothers and I all had our own cars, although I was not allowed to use mine—one of the conditions of my grounding.

The cars were a condition of our moving out to the country northeast of the city, some distance from our home and friends in Toronto. When we were old enough to drive, my dad had promised we would get cars. We weren't going to be trapped, he'd assured us. A bribe had been necessary at that point. It was our second move in five years, and my older brother and I were getting fed up.

After completing the construction of our new home in the suburbs, my dad had decided to leave his job and start his own telecommunications business. My parents had sold the house at a profit, and moved us to Toronto, where an elderly uncle of my mother's sold us his bungalow and moved himself into a senior's residence.

This new home was considerably smaller. Yellowed by nicotine and packed to the ceilings with old newspapers, rusted cans of soda, hat boxes full of matchbooks and other mementos, the house was spavined by neglect. There was a family of racoons living in the chimney, and my bedroom window overlooked a cemetery where my mother told me we had family buried. Garter snakes ran rampant in the yard. It required an adjustment, and adjust we did. My brothers and I started school, and made new friends. My father established the business, hired a small team of engineers, and brought my mom on board to help with administration.

Most of the problems with the house were merely cosmetic. Within two years my parents had it repainted and repaired. Then they put the house up for sale, and we were told we were moving again. This time, to a ten-acre Christmas tree farm forty-five minutes north of Toronto where they built a 4,000-square-foot home. It was an ark in the middle of the ocean.

If I don't remember how I reacted to being told we were going to move the previous time, it's likely because I didn't care. I was too young to care. We'd actually already moved a couple times before my parents built the house in the suburbs. My parents were always on the lookout for better ways to invest and live.

My father would say that the moves were motivated by wanting to provide the best life for my mother, a girl from a middle-class family who always felt inferior and out of place growing up amidst the luxury of Toronto's more affluent Leaside neighbourhood. He'd say he wanted to provide the best life for us, and the city had too many corrupting influences.

My mother would say that this drive was all my father; he was a poor kid from impoverished and pock-marked Tehran. My father is the son of Ali, a farmer who didn't live in the city most of the year, but worked their property in Gorgon, and Ahktar, who married him at fifteen, and had many children, six of whom survived infancy. My Ameh Soroor was the second youngest. My father was the baby of the family. Stories of their early life seem at once grand and absurd. They include the violence and crime that usually accompany poverty. The most memorable story for me involves my father and his cousins stealing a human skull from a cemetery that had flooded. They hid it at my dad's house in a box on top of the kitchen cabinets. It stayed there until his mother found it, and horrified, told him to take it back. She then made the trip to their mosque and gave money they couldn't spare to the collection.

"She prayed," my dad had said, laughing. "She prayed for God to forgive me."

And the skull: He didn't return it to the cemetery. Instead, he and his cousins wrapped the box in pretty paper and a bow, and left it on a bus. It was around the Persian New Year, when gifts were frequently being exchanged. They hoped someone would be delighted with the discovery of a misplaced present.

"That poor woman." He always concluded the story this way, his laughter dying down. My dad would say: "That poor woman," and he'd smile sadly, shaking his head, clucking his tongue. "We didn't make it easy for her."

My father says that his mother and I look a lot alike. He kept a picture of his mother on his nightstand. It was not proper to have the picture out and on display for anyone to see—since his mother was not wearing a chador—but he did let me look at it. I can see our resemblance.

The curve of our cheekbones, sullen set of the mouth, and my middle name is her name. Ahktar. It means star.

Ahktar died before I was born. The cause of death was heart disease, due in part to her heavy smoking. I grew up with this narrative around cigarettes, and it had its intended effect: I thought smoking was dangerous and stupid. So I didn't take to smoking naturally, but when I eventually did start, I made up for my lack of innate enthusiasm with forced, spiteful vigour. I had just gotten out of a month-long house arrest for smoking, although, in fact, I had never smoked before. I had come home from one too many nights out with friends smelling of cigarette smoke. My father may have moved us out of the city to get us away from bad influences, but when it comes to teenagers, there is perhaps no influence worse than too much boredom. And in the country, there were a lot of bored teenagers. Smoking was something to do. There was no telling my father it wasn't something I did, though. He'd decided that I was a smoker and a liar.

I had no say over who I was.

Being grounded when you live in the country is different from being grounded in the city. There's nothing to remind you that you're not alone. There's the arthritic earth, the fish-bone evergreens clustered too close together to thrive, and at night, a sky distended with stars. There's no sidewalk outside your house: no-one to watch walk down the street on their way to school or work or wherever it is that people go. There is no sign of another life, some reassurance by proxy that nothing ends when your hope does. I had a lot of time to be alone and think. I thought about my father, about the reasons he gave us for moving the family out there. It started as a feeling then more than anything else, but I came to see my isolation as a sign that I was always going to be punished for something I hadn't done yet or might never do. I came to understand that there was something dormant and dangerous in me— that I couldn't be trusted.

This uneasy feeling was compounded by the fact my mother had recently told me that father had started tapping our home phone lines and recording our conversations. He had told her that he was only listening to the kids' conversations, but she knew he was listening to her phone calls too. He was convinced we were hiding things, plotting with friends—to have sex, hide money, do drugs.

"Just be careful of what you say on the phone," my mom said. I racked my brain, replaying conversations with friends over and over. What had I done to make my father suspicious of me? Admitted to a friend that I liked a boy? Maybe. Maybe that had been enough.

I started smoking. If it had been my older brother who'd found me out, I might have been quietly scolded, and simply warned. But it wasn't. It was my younger brother. He was the only one of us kids who'd adopted any of my father's cultural notions. Maybe it was because my father only really started extolling them when my older brother and I approached adolescence, and began cultivating lives outside of our immediate family. So perhaps being exposed at a younger age than us made my younger brother more receptive. Maybe not.

Yes, we were vaguely aware we were being raised as Muslim. We knew my mother had converted to Islam when she married my father, but her values were, in every other way, the same semi-practicing Presbyterian ones with which she was raised. We saw my father pray when he was home, but at that time, it was a game: a chance to crawl up on his back and let him rock us back and forth. And there was one trip to a Mosque for a funeral, but there was precious little other influence. I was aware of religion in the same way one might be aware that there's vermiculite in the attic; you know it's there, but it doesn't affect your life unless someone starts disturbing it. Eventually, someone did.

We didn't disturb it on purpose, though. By the time we were preteens, my father saw us growing up in a manner he didn't approve of, especially me. My brothers may have had idiot friends, but apparently such is to be expected of boys. I had friends who were wearing crop-tops and bodysuits as early as grade six. I had friends who had older brothers in high school. I had friends whose parents let them have mixed-sex birthday parties in their basements. My brothers did too, but that was beside the point.

When we'd been introduced to the Quran as young children, my older brother had dismissed it entirely. I had a fledgling academic interest in it, and my younger brother took to it wholly. So perhaps our inclination toward religion was a matter of age. Perhaps it was a matter of personality. Or maybe it was both, but my younger brother was fourteen years old when he discovered me smoking, and was of the perfect age and temperament to be outraged on principle. He'd seen what I was doing, ran up the driveway, screaming for my mom, who was home, and my dad, who was at work. I'd sat on the moss-moulted earth, finished my cigarette and calmly watched him.

My mother, predictably, was far less worried about my smoking than my father. While she by no means approved of smoking, she didn't see it as a sign of my eternal damnation or of her shortcomings as a parent. She asked for my cigarettes and lighter, and threw them away. Then she called my father at work and told him.

"So he'll have time to calm down," she said. He was coming straight home.

My Ameh Soroor gleaned what had happened. I lay my head on her lap and she stroked my hair. She kept stroking when my father walked through the door, and through his anticipated swells of fury and indignation.

"What did I do to deserve this?" he'd asked, addressing no one in particular. "What did I do to God to deserve such a disrespectful daughter?"

I don't know where my mom went while this was happening. When my Ameh had taken to comforting me, she'd disappeared. I didn't think anything of it. She was, I guessed correctly, trying to avoid being caught in the cross-fire. It was my Western friends, my Western vices, my Western mother that was ruining me. My father ranted.

I watched the squat mantel clock behind my father's head tick off ten minutes. At this point, my Ameh held up her hand.

"Bas kon," she said. "Beshin." Stop. Sit down.

He'd had his tirade, and it was over. She was his older sister, and it was time to listen. He tried to interrupt, but she increased her volume, almost imperceptibly, and continued speaking, undaunted.

What I understood: My Ameh was reminding him of all the stupid things he'd done as a teenager. She was counting them off using her free hand: getting into street fights, getting into trouble at school, petty-theft. There was more, but she was speaking quickly, and I had trouble understanding the words.

When she finished, my dad exhaled emphatically, and ran his hands through his hair, messing up the perfectly slicked back coif he'd nurtured past the threat of extinction with daily applications of Rogaine.

He said, in English: "I'm just trying to raise her to be a strong Muslim girl."

His sister replied, in Farsi: "Then you should have raised her in a strong Muslim country."

Family folklore depicts my Amehs as famously fierce. One beat a Morality Officer with a radio antenna from a nearby car after he'd reprimanded her for walking out of her door with a bit of her hairline exposed. Another, whose husband had hit her, grabbed him by the balls and told him she'd cut them off if he touched her again. The Ameh who was arrested for beating the officer was left by her husband in jail for the night to teach her a lesson. And I don't know whether the other Ameh's husband ever did hit her again. But I know that I was in awe of these women, whom my father's culture often portrayed as meek, subservient creatures to be pitied.

My Ameh stopped stroking my hair. "*Bia, joon,*" she said. *Come, my dear.*

I sat up and turned to her.

"Is okay," she said, smiling and tucking my hair behind my ear. She nodded her head in the direction of my father. He was standing, arms slack at his sides, his hair sticking out at odd angles. His moustache drooped, pulling down the corners of his mouth.

I got up and went to him.

"I'm sorry, Dad," I said, leaning into his chest. My Ameh joined the hug, wrapping her arms around us both. She jostled us up and down until we all started laughing. She caught my eye and winked.

I think she knew that I wasn't sorry for smoking.

"Good," my dad said, breaking the embrace to look at me. "In future, you'll see I know you better than even you know yourself."

I was sorry that this would likely be a memorable first of many disappointments for us both. My Ameh glanced back and forth between my father and I. She hadn't understood the English, and was trying to read our expressions. For her sake, I smiled.

For her sake, I also agreed to join them for dinner out that night rather than staying at home by myself.

"You come?" she'd asked.

I shrugged.

"Yes," she said. "You come."

At dinner, she ordered me my favourite dish: *Joojeh*. Saffron chicken. As we were leaving the restaurant, my brothers said goodbye. My older brother said he'd be gone until sometime the next afternoon.

Even if I hadn't been grounded, this is something I'd never have been allowed to do: announce I was going to be gone all night. I would have had to ask, and then I would have been made to assure and re-assure for the next hour that the kids I was going to be with were good kids, from good families. I would have had to explain that a parent would be home. And then I still might not have been permitted to go. Are the parents doctors? Lawyers? Engineers? But to my older brother, my dad simply nodded yes, and my brothers were off. I didn't feel anger toward them; I was simply envious.

I climbed back into the SUV, laden with everyone's leftovers: Styrofoam containers of rice and kabob *koobedieh* coating the enclosed space with a pungent blanket of onion, garlic, and ground beef. It was all too depressing. My mood must have dropped perceptibly because by the time we were pulling out of the restaurant parking lot my Ameh had goaded my dad into translating a story for me. It was about a day they had spent at the lake a few weeks earlier, and judging by my dad's reluctance to tell it, I knew it had to be crude.

I leaned forward, anticipating the story.

My dad explained: "I was driving a boat on the lake and the water was rough. We hit a big wave and your Ameh flew up into the air, and landed on her ass."

My Ameh continued, in a flurry of Farsi that was too fast for me to pick out any meaning, but something she said had everyone in the car erupting in laughter. I was laughing too because whatever my Ameh had said made my dad turn bright red and her sisters whoop in delight. My mom had been quiet all night. I hadn't noticed until seeing that she remained resolutely unmoved in the midst of the hilarious upheaval around her. I tried to see her face, but she'd turned it toward her window.

I turned my attention back to the story.

"What?" I had to know, especially since one of the sisters was now crying with laughter. "What? What? What did she say?"

My Amehs all spoke at once. *Targomeh! Targomeh! Translate! Translate!*

He continued to shake his head, so I decided to entreat my Amoos. I singled out the one seated in front of me, the one who had wine with dinner.

"Please!" I whispered, leaning forward in my seat. "Just tell me!"

He kept his eyes straight ahead, but spoke out of the side of his mouth. "She said: 'If my vagina had teeth, that fall on my ass would have knocked them all out.'"

I let out a staccato snort, choking down the laughter when my dad's eyes met mine in the rearview mirror. *If my vagina had teeth.* I didn't have a clue what it meant, but years later, in my postcolonial literature class in university, I'd learn one interpretation. Vaginal teeth are a symbol with conflicting meanings: It is a defence of women's sexuality, but also a way of demonizing it.

When I'd read about this, I remembered my Ameh's story and wondered if she'd been trying to show that she sympathized with me, that she understood that women have to deal with impossible expectations.

Knowing what I know now—that all of my Amehs had limited education—I wonder whether she'd have even known about this symbolism, or whether it was just a bit of commonplace crass imagery.

That evening, as we drove home, I had a perturbing image of vaginal teeth in my head, and Farsi in my ears. I snuggled into my Ameh's side and listened. As they talked and the night set in, I saw my mother's reflection become increasingly clear in her window. She was so fist-faced that she looked as if she had swallowed her lips.

"ENGLISH!"

Silence. Our eyes turned to my mother. Her body seemed to vibrate.

"Speak English," she said, lowering her voice and straightening herself in her seat. She stretched her neck, first to one side, then the other. It was a movement with which she'd likely intended to suggest ease, but it made her look stiff—practiced.

Everyone stayed quiet. My dad shook his head, then turned the Persian pop music back on. My Ameh Soroor closed her eyes and took a deep breath, deep enough to inhale the music. Her body began to sway slightly, back and forth with the song. She looked at me out of the corner of her eye and smiled; an impish, impervious grin that I would later recognize in my daughter. Nothing could touch her. She started to clap her hands. She started to wiggle her hips.

Swiss Dot

ROO'S FRONT TEETH are beginning to cross, but I can't bring myself to take her thumb out of her mouth. She's finally back to sleep after a fitful night. It's 5:49 a.m., and now Joe and Nuala are up, circling my feet like minnows. It feels like there's a fist in my throat. Nuala's already nattering at me about the outfit I've picked out for her. She doesn't want to wear the floral print dress. She wants the new dress I bought her for Nourouz, the Persian New Year. Held on the first day of spring every year, Nourouz is the Iranian equivalent of Christmas: a highly anticipated celebration with feasts, parties, and presents—especially clothing. Nuala's new dress is a pastel purple party dress with a large cream sash around the middle that ties in an elaborate bow about the size of her torso.

In her search for this one dress, she ripped several others off their hangers. Now, her closet is a disaster, and there's a ticking in my head.

I snap at Nuala, sending her scurrying back to her room to hang her clothes up, which, of course, she can't. She's too little, and she also broke the plastic hangers trying to tug the clothes down. I knew this, and I told her to do it anyway.

My heart hurts and my brain is beginning to itch. I have to try to calm down. I repeat to myself: None of this is a big deal. None of this matters. Clothing on the floor, toothpaste globs in the bathroom sink, a shrivelled pea under the dining room table from last night's dinner

—it's just everyday stuff. I can handle it. I should be able to handle it. Repeat, repeat, repeat for as long as possible: *It's nothing, it's nothing, it's nothing.*

I'm nothing.

I'm struggling to keep this internal war from breaking out and burning the world around me. Even though I logically understand that a little mess won't hurt, reasoning doesn't help. I know, for instance, that it's not logically possible for fire to exist in the vacuum in which I live, and yet it does. I'm burning.

It's difficult to understand, unless you have suffered yourself, or unless you're close to someone who has suffered, and you have held their hand through a hell only they could experience. Unless you believe them when they tell you it's there.

And it is there. Some days, I manage to keep its boundaries contained. Some days, its lines advance, expand. Sometimes, I lose.

I'm losing today, and I'm taking it hard because I'd convinced myself that I'd done everything to make sure I wouldn't. I'd gone to bed early. I'd slept in gym shorts and a training top so I could roll out of bed and pump endorphins into my body before the kids got up, before my mind woke up, and before it started in on me again—the morning's insistent chattering and the crows picking at dawn in my backyard. The clothes-hangers scraping across a metal clothing rod and the cat licking crumbs off the toaster. There's tiny jam hand print on the fridge door. A lopsided heart drawn in the condensation on the dining room window. A school lunch bag on the counter, open and unpacked. From Nuala's room comes the sound of her sniffling.

Nuala once told me that she had a dream of me burning all her dresses and baby dolls. "But I know it was a dream, Mommy. You love me too much to do that." I nod my head yes, of course, and hope she really believes that. I picture her dolls—all the toys in our house— aflame in a glorious blaze and feel my eyes water with relief. I take a deep breath in, and exhale slowly.

I didn't buy Nuala her first doll until she was two. I thought about all the preferences that are regularly foisted on children: boys like blue and playing rough with trucks; girls like pink and playing mommy with dolls. So, until she was two, Nuala played with the same toys as her brother: puzzles, blocks, cars, animal figurines, teddy bears. But when she got that doll, her world changed. She mothered it, wrapping it in blankets, putting it down for naps, and kissing its boo-boos. And she undoubtedly loves pink, despite my tendency to buy clothes in neutral colours. Of course, many kids are forced into wearing clothes and playing with toys they don't connect with, but pink is Nuala's truth. And I have to tell myself to remember this. I never want her to feel frivolous or stupid because of who she is.

I check on Roo. She's still sleeping, dark blond hair curling around her ears like seafoam, the cat snuggling at the foot of the crib. She's not sucking her thumb, thank God. Our family dentist has assured me that some thumb-sucking at this age likely won't warp her bite. Still, I cringe every time she puts her thumb in her mouth. My teeth have been the only near-perfect thing in my life. Absolutely straight. No cavities. Until recently, I've clung to this natural gift.

A few months ago, I noticed a hairline crack in one of my front teeth. Since then, it has entirely chipped off—less than a millimeter where the two front teeth meet. For the first couple of weeks, I'd run my tongue over my tooth, jamming it into the sharp edge of the chip so it bled.

My dentist said the chip is likely the result of the enamel on the back of my teeth deteriorating over the years.

"Probably because … well, after years of acid wear, and …" She trailed off.

"Because of my bulimia," I said. I'd been upfront with her about it. The damage was so obvious.

"Yes."

I told my mother about my tooth, and about how I was going to get it fixed when my fillings were going to be done.

"Fillings?" She was incredulous. "You have cavities?"

"No, not cavities," I explained. I needed fillings to patch over the nerves that have been exposed due to aggressive brushing. I had to keep perfect the one perfect thing I had.

"Well, either way, you've ruined them." She sighed dramatically.

I know she's teasing me, but I also know she's right. I ruined them.

Dreaming that your teeth fall out or crumble is one of the most common dreams. It's supposed to mean that you are feeling anxious about a loss of power, or attractiveness, or about having said something foolish. This, unsurprisingly, is my most frequently recurring dream.

Joe is standing at the end of the hall, huge brown eyes watching me as I close Roo's bedroom door, gently, not shutting it entirely, so I can hear her if she wakes up.

"Mommy," he whispers, "can I talk to you for a second?"

Joe, seven years old, is my sweet, big boy. When I don't want to play dinosaurs or roughhouse with him, he doesn't press me. He repeats what he has heard his dad say: "Mommy's for kisses and cuddles." This is something I've said as well, but I've got to be good for something else.

Joe has a face that escapes me these days, like the sound of the ocean in a wind tunnel. How it goes around or over, how it comes down and across. There are days when he's here, but I don't see him at all. I crouch down so we're at eye level. He wants to know if jaguars are better swimmers than lions. He's clutching a few figurines from his Schleich big cats collection in his arms.

"Don't know," I say. "What do you think?"

He smiles and shrugs, rubbing his cheek against mine before walking off.

My mind's been muddled by lullabies.

I've forgotten about Nuala. She's still in her room. I stand at the door and watch her trying to shove her dresses in between the other clothes hanging in her packed closet. Outside her window, there's a cottontail cloudscape. I want to bring it to my face, inhale it until my insides are vapour.

When I was around Nuala's age, I couldn't settle down until everything in my closet was perfectly arranged and tucked away. Even after I tidied and shut the door, I'd lie in bed obsessing until I checked on it again; and then I'd re-arrange something else. I hated that I couldn't stop doing this. I couldn't help it, either. The thought of one jean leg hanging out of the laundry basket, or a single dress not in line with the others would prevent me from falling asleep.

At that early stage in my life, my parents weren't aware of these obsessions of mine, or if they were, they would have likely considered them a personality quirk. It would be years before I tried to tell my parents about how a mess around the house was shattering to me.

I lean against the doorframe, feeling heavy and slack. Nuala's head and most of her torso have been consumed by the mass of clothing in her closet. Only her bottom and legs stick out, wiggling around as she struggles to hang dresses. When I was her age, I also used to write over my friends' messy birthday greetings in the cards they gave me in my own, meticulous penmanship. I used thick marker over pen and pencil to try to cover up their shaky, uncertain handwriting. I couldn't stand the look of it. This undertaking was a once-a-year chore. The closet— that was a daily struggle. I couldn't avoid having to get dressed. Every day I'd need to go in there and disrupt the order I had tried to impose.

Not that I ever had as many clothes to contend with as Nuala—definitely not as many dresses. Although my mother started a fashion line called *Klassy Kids*, and although I modelled dresses that would make Nuala weep for joy—white lace, green silk, and my favourite, a blush Swiss Dot party dress—I never got to keep the dresses. They were made to be sold. My mother did make me other dresses, though. They were never as fancy or frilly as the ones I modelled, and never as many as in my daughter's closet, but she did make me dresses. They were beautiful, yes, but more subdued. Maybe I never asked for a more ornate dress. Maybe I did but she didn't have time to make it. My mother's business did well, but my mom—a stay-at-home parent of three—became overwhelmed and eventually abandoned the line. My dad had wanted her to stick it out, not only to keep her busy while we kids were at school and he was overseas on trips, but also to bring in some extra money.

We'd just moved from North York, where we were all born, to a developing suburb of Toronto. My parents hired architects and contractors, and had our new house built from scratch. It was expensive and big, and it needed to be furnished. I can't imagine that the money from *Klassy Kids* earned my mother very much, especially knowing the amount of effort that went into making the clothing. I often fell asleep to the sound of her sewing machine echoing up the cavernous stairwell to my bedroom. I would wake in the middle of the night and hear it still humming. The profits from her creations simply didn't justify the time and effort stitched into each garment, but I know that money was an issue. What I mean to say is that I know this now.

Back then, all I knew was the word 'mortgage'. We'd moved when I was five, and I didn't know what mortgage meant, but it was one of those words you overhear as a child that doesn't have to carry a clear meaning to have weight. You glean a meaning by watching the word in action: the way it elicits reaction, and the precise reaction it elicits. You learn.

Mortgage, I learned, was not a good word, and I learned like this: There was a call from my dad, who was in Hong Kong, or Singapore, or Jakarta, or somewhere else his job as a telecommunications engineer took him. My mom answered. It was just after lunch, so it was either during summer vacation or on a weekend. The afternoon pushed through our large windows, illuminating the family room in floating gold dust. My brothers and I were watching *The Flintstones*—my older brother on his stomach on the floor, his chin cupped in his hands, and my younger brother and I crammed together on a wooden rocking chair. We didn't rock, though, not on this chair, because when it went back it felt like it was going to go back forever.

On TV, Pebbles and Bamm-Bamm were at a birthday party. I sucked on the insides of my cheeks. The sticky sweetness of a peanut butter and strawberry jam sandwich lingered.

My mom was on the phone with my dad in the kitchen, and she was getting louder; her words were hurried. I heard her say *mortgage* and my guts clenched. Because my brother and I were wedged in the chair, I had to strain to turn around to see her.

"You can't buy that! How are we going to pay the mortgage?" She was pacing, reined in every few steps by the limits of the telephone cord. She caught me looking at her and held my gaze, while listening to whatever my dad was saying.

I smiled, trying to make her smile.

She clenched her free hand into a fist and turned away. "But we don't *need* it!"

I turned back to the TV and the chair rocked back with my weight.

My brother stiffened, grabbing the arm of the chair and my leg to steady himself.

"Sorry," I whispered, and we waited out the rocking. In the kitchen, my mom slammed down the phone. That night, I had dreamed that the wrought iron door knob in my bedroom had melted and turned into an enigmatic running man. I woke up calling for my mom, but she didn't hear me over the mechanical drone of the sewing machine.

Or, she heard me, and didn't come. I remember yelling for her so loudly.

———⊷ I'm watching Nuala and I can't breathe. Her fair skin is getting flushed, and she's frustrated because the dresses won't stay up. "Come on, come on!" She pleads under her breath.

Sometimes, when one of the kids calls me, I pretend I don't hear. They need so much, and some days I have nothing to give.

"Nuala," I say gently, going over to her and guiding her out of the closet. "Just leave it, okay? I'll fix it. Gramps will be here to pick Roo up soon, and you need to get ready for school. Come eat."

She sighs. "Okay, Mommy." And leans in for a hug. There's never a bad time for hugs, I always tell them, and I make sure to honour this, no matter how strung out I feel. I hold her close, breathing in the bubble gum body wash from her bath last night, and it breaks my heart that I have her. I don't deserve her—not one blond hair on her head. I make sure to hold her until she's ready to let go.

Over breakfast she quizzes me about my wedding day. Joe has long since finished, cleared his place, and gone to play in his room.

"Did you kiss Daddy?"

"Yes."

"Did you wear a big dress?"

"No."

"Why not?"

"I didn't want one."

"I like big dresses."

"I know you do."

"Where's your dress now?"

"In my closet."

"Can I see it?"

"Not now. Please eat."

"Did it have flowers on it?"

"No."

"Why? I love flowers."

"I know."

She already knows almost everything about my wedding day. She has asked me about it, many times before.

"Did your mommy make your dress?"

"Yes, bug."

"Will you make me my wedding dress?"

"If you want."

I make a promise to myself to make Nuala another dress for Nourouz—something handmade, something she can keep, look at, and know that I made it for her because I love her so much. I'm not as talented at sewing as my mother, despite her best efforts to teach me, but my skills would do. I would make Nuala a dress in any colour, any style she wants. I make a lot of promises like this every single morning, lying in bed, before I've opened my eyes or had to talk to anyone. I promise to do better. Be better. I promise that I won't raise my voice or be short tempered. I promise that I'll be kinder to everyone today, including myself.

"Mommy, I want my wedding dress to be like yours."

"Maybe not when you grow up." I'd said the same thing to my mom when I was a little girl.

"Yes, I will," she insists, talking to me through a mouth full of cereal. She pauses to swallow, then continues: "Was your dress a pretty princess dress?"

"It was a pretty dress, yes, but not a princess dress."

"What kind of dress was it?"

"Nuala, honey, for the love of God—you may not even want to get married!"

"Was the dress lace?"

"No, eyelet. Nuala, please just eat."

"What's eyelet?"

When I was a child thinking of my wedding day, I thought I'd ask my mother to make me a Swiss Dot dress. This is a delicate sheer cotton fabric embellished with small dots at regular intervals, and usually used for baby clothes, wedding dresses, or curtains. This was all I wanted. The busy, perfectly ordered elegance of the pattern soothed my mind. It still does.

———• When the time came for me to get married, I wasn't thinking about Swiss Dot. I had forgotten about it. I asked my mother to make me a satin, backless dress that I ended up not wanting to wear because I was unexpectedly pregnant with Joe. It pulled across my hips, revealing a tight, impossible bump.

I cried for hours after my first fitting. Afterwards, my mother suggested scrapping the satin dress altogether and taking another approach. We agreed on a flowing eyelet gown with satin trim. It actually ended up looking a little like my mother's wedding dress: a throwback to the 1970s, empire waist with discreet and whimsical lines, and a slimming focal point.

I tried it on a few days ago, when my husband was out grocery shopping with the kids. I couldn't get it to zip up past my breasts, which have grown two sizes since I had my children. My right foot had grown an entire size, too, while I was pregnant with Nuala. But the real reason the dress wouldn't do up was not only the size of my breasts. I've gained forty pounds since Roo was born, thanks to booze, medications, and sleepless nights. I stood in front of the full-length mirror in my bedroom, my unzipped dress gapping at the back, and my stomach bulging at the front, as I fought back tears. I clenched my lips and told myself: Don't you dare cry. You have no one to blame but yourself.

———• Nuala's still romanticizing my past and her future, and I can't stand that either, so I get up while she's still talking and start picking dead leaves off the plant by the kitchen window. I toss a tangle of rot into the compost, and turn off the light above the sink. I stare out into the backyard. Even with the window closed, I can hear the blackbirds screaming in the trees. Nuala chatters on and I open the window to drown her out. The cat has snuck out of Roo's room and is circling my legs, begging loudly for treats. I roll my shoulders back and try to stand up straighter. Best way to instantly lose ten pounds. You cow.

The cat keeps meowing.

"Oh, shut up," I mumble, slamming shut the window.

I make myself sick.

———→ Roo wakes, and my father arrives, all moustache tickle kisses and fart jokes for the kids. He and my mother are going to take Roo for the day, so I can have some time to myself; to work, sleep, stare at the wall.

"Whatever you need to do," my mom had said. "Just take the time and enjoy it." I'd argued against it, not wanting to admit I needed help, but my dad said he was coming anyway.

I'd opened the front door and he wrapped me in a hug before the storm door could close behind him. He smelled of diesel fuel and grease remover—a familiar aura from his habitual tinkering on cars. I rested my head against his shoulder, felt a knot in my mind loosen. Just a little.

"It's okay, Bear," he'd said, using the pet name he'd given me as a child. "Relax today."

My dad helps the older two get ready for school, while Roo, who takes awhile to wake up and disconnect from me, sits on my lap and eats a banana. She tucks her free hand into the front of my shirt and snuggles into my chest; her rosebud curls tickle my nose. There's her warm, sweet toddler scent. There are some days I'm so touched out I want to scream.

Nuala has given up on me and is trying to get Gramps to find her Nourouz dress. He unearths it from the crowd of dresses in her closet after five minutes of searching, after I've dismissed his pleas for assistance.

"Dad, seriously," I said. "She's just going to ruin it at school, and then I'm going to have to try to get all the stains out or buy her another dress. You're not helping. You're just giving me one more thing that I'll have to do!"

He ignores me, helps Nuala get changed, and entices Roo away with marshmallows he carries in his shirt pocket. He says he'll walk the kids to school.

"No, Dad. I'll come."

"You stay," he says, putting one hand up and blocking my way out the front door. "I'll walk the babies." And just like that, they're gone. I stand there a moment, trying to acclimatize myself to the silence. My ears strain, my eyes dart around the empty foyer. I spot Nuala's water bottle. She's forgotten it on the front hall table. I run out after them, sprinting across the lawn and down the sidewalk in my bare feet.

I catch Nuala, hugging her tight and kissing her face, her head. I tuck her water bottle into her backpack, and promise myself that I'll put on the necklace she got me for Mother's Day. I'll do it before she gets home. It's a heart-shaped locket and the inscription reads "Mom". I haven't been able to bring myself to wear it since she gave it to me. I don't want, don't deserve it.

I pull Nuala close again. "I love you, I love you, I love you," I murmur into her hair.

She pushes away, looks at me hard, then nods. "When I get to school, I'll draw you something nice."

Once alone in the house again, I open my grandmother's cedar chest and look at the fabric and patterns I'd begged off my mother with every intention of starting to sew for the kids. I pick out a bolt of ivory Swiss Dot, and a pattern for a girl's summer dress with criss-cross straps and faux-pearl buttons down the back. I'm out of my league, but I go back to the front hall closet and unearth my sewing machine, heavy and hulking, stashed away in the corner.

I move aside the shoe rack and crouch down to yank it out. I tug hard, lose my grip, and fall onto the rack, sending shoes spilling onto the floor, knocking coats down from the hangers. I lie there, flat on my back and I tell myself not to think of the mess. I feel as if I'm turning molten inside. I try to let it flow out of me. I picture a paper boat bobbing atop a river of lava, sparks flitting around like fireflies. But the boat—it's okay.

I lie there and let it drift, will it to stay drifting. The cat comes over and licks my eyebrows, so I act cat to achieve cat status. That glazed know-it-all wonder.

I close my eyes and envision the dress I'll make for Nuala: the shiny, smooth, spherical buttons, the waves in the full skirt, the precise intervals between the thousands of tiny dots. I tell myself that I'll start on it today. I tell myself it will be beautiful. I tell myself that it will never be a lack of anything that kills me.

I'm Still Gone

WE WERE WALKING in the rain, this guy and I. I'd just met him at a campus party and didn't know his name—didn't know or couldn't remember.

"Ben?" I guessed.

He'd said: "No, and I'm not telling you again." Even though, like I said, I wasn't convinced he had told me in the first place.

I shrugged. "Suit yourself!" Because it made no difference to me anyway. He could have been anyone. I was just a girl with a buzz and a hacksaw heart looking to disappear, and I needed someone to help make that happen. The night before it had been someone else. Tonight, this guy.

And man, *this guy*.

In my blackout twenties, there were a lot of guys, but this one had the greenest eyes I'd ever seen. For the first few minutes we talked, I thought his eyes were blue because he carried himself like a man with blue eyes, with that distant ease. But no. His eyes were green, all shades of green, really, like a rainforest. He took my hand when we crossed the street, and my soul turned to steam. I could feel it: Where I ended and where the world began was getting less clear.

It had been my idea to leave the party. I'd been bored, but mostly I'd wanted to leave because the only booze they had left was beer, and that had too many calories. I was already feeling squeezed into my pants.

"Hope you don't mind that I wanted to leave," I'd said as we walked to his car. He'd parked it in a municipal lot, a couple blocks away.

"Not at all," he said. "I'd been there too long anyway. That was my buddy's place. How do you know him?"

"I don't know." I'd been invited by a friend of a friend. That friend was still there, presumably.

"You don't know how you know him?"

"I mean, I don't know him. At all."

He smiled, and it was as soft as snow, as easy and incessant.

"What *do* you know?"

I told him that he walked like a little boy, and he said: "Do not."

He did.

It was one of the first things I'd noticed about him. His right foot was slightly more turned in than his left, and he moved through space as though he was reinventing it. I found this gentle, haphazard approach to motion reassuring: I saw it as a sign that there can be imperfection and perfection all at once.

I'd needed this comfort. I'd spent the day trying to fight through a hangover caused by the previous night's partying. I was learning that you can't fill the void. You can only feed it.

I knew that no amount of time at the gym would fix that feeling, so I'd skipped my workout, loaded up on fast food, and sequestered myself in my apartment. There, I spent the rest of the day eating and purging and eating and purging and eating and eating until my face and body were bloated and my stomach ached and my throat burned and I thought I'd die or never, ever, ever do this again. Whichever came first, or both. At one point, I clogged the toilet and resorted to throwing up in a grocery bag.

I knew I wouldn't win if I kept drinking like I was, but that didn't stop me. The small amount of relief afforded by even a few hours of oblivion was worth the consequences. I couldn't see a puddle without feeling an ocean. I didn't know of another way to deal with the hugeness of these pressing emotions. All the hate, fear, longing, frustration, and sadness. All my unclaimed life; it was passing me by and I had no way to stop it. I had nothing but a laundry list of neuroses and a plastic bag of vomit.

When a friend called around 7 p.m. to invite me to a party, she'd offered a break from thinking about all these things. I'd looked at the half-full bottle of vanilla-flavoured vodka on my counter that I'd been avoiding all day, and thought: *Why the hell not?* There was always something to prove—to myself, to someone else. I was tired of having to try to prove I was worthy of trust, consideration, love. It was easier to just not be worth the effort.

I'd poured myself a drink, raised a glass and thought: *Drink 'til your hot.*

"Suffering produces endurance, endurance produces character, and character produces hope," I said.

The guy laughed. "Do you know where that's from?"

"Dunno. I just know it. Sounds like Thomas Hardy."

"It's from the bible."

"Then why did you ask me, if you knew?"

"I wanted to see if *you* knew."

"I'm Muslim. I don't do the Bible." I'd smiled at myself. It was amazing: We were drifting through our soundstage city, street lights bouncing off glistening pavement toward the sky; it was amazing that I could be with this guy, who was unloading his gaze on me, but still drift in and out, in and out of myself as I pleased.

I learned how to exist outside my body early in life. In my 1997 high school yearbook, a boy had drawn a picture of a three-humped camel with horns, tail lifted, shitting a turban shaped coil. He'd written, "Turban Maker" underneath. I didn't understand. I was half-Iranian Muslim, not a Sikh. I was born and raised in Canada, and my mom was sixth-generation Canadian, and of British descent. He showed his friends his work, and they laughed, so when he handed me my book back, I laughed too.

Without sufficient acuity to be offended, I was embarrassed instead. I knew I'd been excluded and pushed to a periphery and fondled into strangeness. But I didn't understand what was happening.

As I was laughing, another boy in the cafeteria narrowly missed tipping his drink over in my lap and made a crack about not wanting to spill his drink on my Persian rug. When I walked down the hall and other kids trilled ululations in my wake, I remember the feeling of being outside of my own body, becoming both spectacle and spectre. It was as if I was watching a scene in a movie. This sudden dissociation—it wasn't easy, but it wasn't that hard either. I was ready to disappear.

I mentioned these experiences to my mother. She told me about how when we first moved to the area and she was carpooling with a group of other women to a school event, one of them—upon learning that my father was Iranian and Muslim—remarked that people who come to Canada should adopt the culture. My mom shrugged. Some people are just small-minded. You can't change it. Besides, my mom had wanted to know, what was wrong with being biracial? Halle Berry was biracial, and she was a serious, successful actress, as well as a beautiful and highly desired woman.

"I'm not Halle Berry," I said. "I'm this." I said, pointing to my ass. "And this," pointing to my nose.

"But we can fix that," my mom said. The bump on my nose was so prominent that it would burn badly in the summer, cracking, peeling, and bleeding. "That can be taken care of."

The plastic surgeon agreed. He broke my nose down the middle to narrow it, and shaved seven millimetres off the top. He said: "Now everyone will finally be able to see your beautiful eyes."

I bought grey coloured contacts, and as for my ass, I started going to the gym. I avoided eating pizza and French fries at lunch with my friends and greasy *shomneh* kabob at home with my family. I ate heads of lettuce, peeling back leaf after leaf and chewing slowly. I ate low-fat cottage cheese, and, for a treat, low-fat York Peppermint Patties. I streaked my hair blonde, waxed my upper lip, plucked my eyebrows to a thin screech.

I worked on making parts of myself disappear to suit my surroundings, the way certain lizards can drop their tails to become lighter, and run faster to survive.

I went to parties, but only with my small, close group of friends. I didn't date boys in my school. The first guy I dated was twenty-one and he lived in another town—a bigger city. I was eighteen and relieved to be able to cross the typical teenage milestones off my list without attracting unwanted attention from my peers or my parents, mostly my father. All the ways in which I was different had already made me the object of too much unwanted attention. I still had to deal with comments at school and suspicion at home, but it was nice to fly under the radar, at least in some areas of my life.

———— "You know," the green-eyed guy said, hooking his arm through mine and pulling me closer, "to know the Bible, you don't have to be Christian."

"Is that your name?"

"What?"

"Christian."

He laughed and rolled his eyes. I'd laughed along too, amused by myself.

His eyes aren't the reason I remember him. They're part of what I recall, but not the part that has made him stand out from all the other guys I've met and forgotten. I'm sure many had beautiful eyes. Beautiful eyes, beautiful smiles, and beautiful bodies. They had a pleasant drugging effect on me. With them, I could hardly feel the brutal rearranging of my skin-deep fragments.

I called these guys whenever I started thinking too much. The guys called me:

Sexy.

Slut.

Snob.

Persian princess.

I knew I couldn't possibly be all these things; being them all meant that I wasn't any of them. I didn't exist. And if I didn't exist, no one could hurt me. You can see the temptation.

It's common to think that girls like me are waiting to be saved—to be swept up, away, and into a love story. This, I think, is a misogynistic view. I wasn't waiting for anyone to fall in love with me, the real me. The real me is the last person I wanted anyone to see. I couldn't stand her. She was the butt of jokes. She was shady. She couldn't be trusted. What I wanted was to experiment with newer, better, possible versions of myself. Think of it as rigorous split audience testing: Which version of me sits better with audiences. How'd you like this? How'd you like me now? More importantly: How did I like the way their liking me made me feel? When I knew a guy was buying into whatever skin I had slipped into, I felt radiantly clever, if just for a little while. It's easy to fall in love with this feeling.

Every new face was a fresh start, a new high.

The reason I remember this new guy was because he saw my many contradictions and he cared enough to call me on them. He and I were walking along and it started misting, a scaly film falling on our hair, on our faces. I was laughing again, gasping for air, because he was making fun of me for my repeated use of the phrase: "In a nutshell."

"All night," he said, "you've been describing yourself 'in a nutshell.'" He stopped, put one hand on his hip and flipped the other one out. Speaking in falsetto he mimicked: "I'm a second-year English major who wants to do a PhD dissertation in postcolonial literature. That's me in a nutshell." "I'm a gym junkie who wants to be a lawyer. That's me in a nutshell." "I love BBC period dramas and don't give a fuck what you or anyone else thinks of me. Me, in a nutshell."

He was right. I had said that—all of it, more or less. I had the verbal incontinence that's typical of classic booze-bender brain. I'd been showering him in a shitstorm of selfs and couldn't decide or remember how I wanted him to perceive me. My words themselves, however, were a clarion. I spoke with pure, anaesthetic lucidity.

"So," he asked, unlocking his car. "which nutshell are you?"

I hated trying to explain.

He opened the door for me.

I hated feeling cleaned out like that.

I cocked my thumbs and pointed them back toward myself. "I'm this nutshell," I winked. "And you ain't gonna crack me."

Even though I don't remember agreeing to go back to his place, it's likely I did because I remember wanting to be with him. Tall, with thickly veined forearms and broad shoulders like angel wings, he was the kind of person I guessed that I could lose myself in. I could see my behaviour was dangerous. The boys, the booze: Someone could hurt me. Or I could hurt myself. I was aware of this, but I didn't care. There was no loss of self to lament.

He could have been anyone, wanted anything. It didn't matter. When you want to be everything and nothing at once, you need to push and push and push until you feel nothing.

We were kissing in his car and the rain was beating bullets on the roof. I had my seatbelt on and was having to strain to be near him. One of his hands was in my hair and the other on the back of my neck, softly. My hands were clenched around the seat belt, and there was a vein pulsing in my neck.

He stopped, pulling back a little so our lips were inches apart.

"Look" he said. I opened my eyes. There was nothing and no one between us except electric wisps, the lingering heat of his mouth on mine, a rawness on my chin from his stubbled jaw.

And one other thing: silence.

He grinned, his forehead resting against mine; his greens eyes, huge and immaculate. "Look. You made it stop raining."

Body Filler

HAIR GROWS AT a rate of half an inch per month. Nothing you can do to change that. Still, Porsche pulled it back into a tight ponytail after showering because she thought it would grow faster. The skin around her hairline was raw from the tension. But she was proud of her hair. Long and red, it was, she said, the most consistent thing in her life.

Porsche was a prostitute.

"Escort," she said, correcting me the first time I used the word. "I mean, yeah, it's pretty much the same thing, but we don't just fuck 'em. Our guys want the girlfriend experience."

"Escort" had been the word used in the classified ad, which had been tucked away in the back of a newspaper. I'd called the service, got the address, and set up a meeting. Escort was the word that had drawn me in. If the ad had called for prostitutes, I would never have inquired. I wasn't totally naïve—I knew that escorts had sex for money. I just hoped that maybe there were some who really just got paid to go on dates with lonely men. As someone practiced in the art of self-deception, I told myself this over and over on the day between making the appointment for my interview and the interview itself. It strengthened my resolve.

Cynthia, the woman who managed the service, took one look at me when I walked through her door and said: "So, tell me your problem."

My ex-boyfriend thought my problem was that I'd never planned my life after university; that I didn't know what I wanted. After graduation, I'd tried to make the boomerang backtrack to my parents' home, but unless I was slinging a shoulder of Smirnoff in my purse, the lack of prospects at my parents' was unbearable. I'd expected to immediately land some prestigious job, but in all my time studying humanities, I hadn't considered any practical application for my degree. This oversight was humiliating, especially since I'd been so confident that I'd chosen the right path by going against my father's wishes by deciding to pursue a life of literature instead of law. I was certain a place in the world would open for me. My degree was supposed to have made me stronger and more assured, but I was more lost than ever.

Then there was my ex-boyfriend. I can't remember whether I ever told him this, but one of the reasons I left my parents and took a job in another city was to be nearer to him. I'd sit on the edge of his bed while he slept, sprawled, and try to imagine his arm outstretched like that for me. Within a few weeks of leaving my parents' home again, he wasn't my boyfriend anymore. It was too much, he'd said. I was too much.

——— I was sitting in front of Cynthia and she was shaking her head knowingly. "Men." Cynthia had a rough, smoker's laugh. "Figures."

But he wasn't the only reason I was there. I was offered a position as a writer for a media company. I thought, finally, my degree and desires would align with my reality. My elation was undercut by my father's suspicions.

"He thinks you're up to something," my mom had said.

"What could I possibly be up to?" I'd asked, but I already knew. It was the same thing my father always thought women were up to when they wanted their independence.

"It's because you mentioned that boy was there," my mom explained. "Your father thinks it's the only reason you went back. Driven by your ... well, I can't say it. But you know."

"My vagina."

"Yes."

"He thinks I'm behaving like a whore."

"Yes."

I felt reduced to a guileless, malleable mound of flesh with doll-hinge legs. I didn't want to believe my father would think these things of me, never mind women in general. But he did. I knew he did, and I knew that no amount of discussion would ever change his mind. I'd tried before, and even as I was talking, I could see that he thought I was spewing lies fuelled by my base biological instinct.

So when the money I was making working as a writer wasn't enough to keep up with payments on my student debt, living expenses, and booze, and when I needed more money but I couldn't ask my dad for help without him telling me I had to come home to get it, I began to get frantic. And not just because I was broke. I'd been a student for years and was used to not having money. A financial crisis alone would not have been enough to make me answer an ad for escorts. It was a combination of every shattered thing: my recent breakup, my drinking, my quarter-life crisis, my eating disorder and my unchecked depression and OCD.

I was a combination of shattered things.

"But mostly, just like I said." Cynthia crushed a half-finished ciga-rette in her ashtray. "*Men.*"

I sat across from a slim, velour-jumpsuit-clad, Cynthia and nod-ded. Yes, men. Cynthia was appraising me with professional coolness. I half expected her to check my teeth and gums. She took a deep breath and narrowed her eyes at me. I was wearing a black V-neck halter top and tight black pants. I thanked God I was always two sizes smaller when I woke up after drinking. I always felt a small triumph when I shimmied into the world, dressed and deflated like that. I smiled at her with a full, toothy grin. She smirked back.

Cynthia didn't just manage the service. She owned it.

"A pimp," Porsche had said, "but don't ever call her that. She doesn't like it, and us girls try to respect one another's pretensions."

Porsche had been assigned by Cynthia to show me around. "Show you the ropes!" Porsche had said, guffawing. "Which incidentally are in the back-hall closet if you need them."

Porsche had also been the one to give me a name, Veronica, like the character from the Archie comic books. "Suits you. A snooty little beauty with dark hair." She laughed, revealing a chipped eyetooth.

"I'm not snooty," I'd shot back, snootily, but I liked the name; it seemed like it belonged to someone who was aloof, cool. I could feel myself slipping away. Maybe, I thought, this was where I was meant to be; bad as it was, it was bound to be easier being bad where I belonged than trying to be good where I didn't.

Being a whore, I thought, would be nothing new for me. That word, the idea it represented, had been embedded in my psyche long before I showed up at Cynthia's door.

————→ According to family legend, I was named after a prostitute, a Turkish hooker my dad had met when he was doing his mandatory military service in Iran. The story goes like this: My mother hadn't known this was my namesake when she agreed to the name. My dad had told her he liked it because he'd known a girl in school by the name, and she'd been beautiful, smart and kind. I can't even remember any longer who told me this story; it was related so long ago, and it seems I've been told it so many times since then that it has become part of my personal narrative. I do remember the tale was supposed to be funny, and it was. My dad, who extolled virtues of modesty and purity in women, named me after a prostitute.

A few years ago, I'd inquired whether the story was true, and my father asked where I'd heard it. His moustache started twitching so fiercely that I just shrugged and didn't answer. And he didn't answer me either. We just stood there, twitching at each other. How did he meet the woman, my next question, ricocheted around in my skull like an errant bullet, rattling my brains until I started laughing—nervously at first, and then with my whole body.

My dad raised an eyebrow. My whole body was convulsing with laughter. He shook his head at me. Crazy girl.

My name means 'mist around the moon.' An abstraction of a natural wonder—something visible but without substance.

Whoever had told me the story about my name was right: it *was* funny.

"Desire," Porsche had said, "is a funny thing."

She was walking me through the job description. "A guy will walk in off the street and you can think you got him pegged by looking at him, but you can never tell what type of girl he'll want, so don't assume."

She pulled her ponytail tighter. Her hair was over-processed, like a doll's hair. It was thinning in some areas as if she'd been loved too much. "And if you want to make good money here, you have to be as many types of girls as possible."

That, I knew, I could do.

———+ The escort service spread out over a large second-hand store on the city's main downtown street. It had a surprising number of rooms, including a common area—furnished with two faux-suede couches, two end tables, and a life-sized cardboard cut-out of Rocky Balboa. Right off the lounge was a kitchen that was occasionally used to pre-pare meals, but more often for smoking and drinking tea. Beside the kitchen was Cynthia's office and a large bathroom for the girls, com-plete with a Jacuzzi and plush cream-coloured bathmats. Clients never saw these areas. Once they were in the lounge, they'd go right, then down an L-shaped hall where there were two deluxe bedroom suites for high-paying in-house customers, five smaller rooms for regular clients, and a well-maintained bathroom with a shower stall, toilet, and sink, also for clients.

———+ Out of the twenty-three girls who worked for Cynthia, I ran into about a third coming in, going out, or sitting around the service during the first and only evening I spent there. I'd come after work at my day job and was to stay the night to see whether I liked it. Other than Porsche, none of the girls spoke to me. I had not expected this— to be shunned.

"Don't take it personally," Porsche said. "It's not that they don't like you, but some girls find this job will drain them dead if they start giving themselves away to everyone who wants a little of their atten-tion. They're just conserving energy."

The next morning, I was woken up by Porsche looking for something in her purse. I'd been sleeping on the couch in the common area. Or trying to. It had been a busy night, which meant that I couldn't use any of the rooms to sleep, which is what Porsche said the girls usually did when it was slow. "As slow as we get," she'd said, winking. Porsche had done an outcall, which she said to do only if you knew the person, and the only way to know the client is if he came here first. This outcall was an 18-year-old guy—a regular. "His parents are out of town," she said. They left their Jag, she'd added, rolling her eyes. "I hope my son won't turn out to be a little shit like that."

"You have a son?" I was genuinely surprised.

She smiled at me; a woodland creature lost in the city.

———+ At around 2 a.m., I'd considered going home to the basement bachelor apartment I was renting to sleep there. It was only a twenty-minute walk away, but I'd been drinking and was to wasted and lonely to want to go anywhere. I'd stayed the whole night, and now Porsche was looming over me wearing jeans, flip-flops, and a tank-top. This was the first time I'd seen her fully dressed, but I didn't think about that right away.

I could tell she wanted to ask me how my night was, but didn't.

"Well, I'm off today!" She said this turning away and waving over her head.

Cynthia arrived shortly after Porsche left. After spending a few minutes behind the locked door of her office, she came out, eyeing me. She asked what Porsche didn't.

"So," she said, taking clean cups out of the draining board and putting them away. "Good night?"

She was eyeing me over her shoulder. I'd gathered enough about Cynthia's business-first acumen by that point to know her question was rhetorical.

I stretched and said: "Mm hm. Yeah, just fine." I looked around for my bottle of water; my head pounded and I was alcohol dehydrated.

"Well, if you've been out here all night," Cynthia glanced around the common area. "I can't see how that could be too good."

During our initial interview, after Cynthia had confirmed her hunch that I was another damaged girl who'd ended up on her door-step because of daddy issues, she asked if I had a university education. I thought it a moot point, given the job for which I was applying, and told her so, but she insisted that it always matters.

"It shows depth of character. Most of the girls here have some post-secondary education." She paused to take a sip of coffee, looking at me over her cup. "Don't act so surprised! You're not so unique after all, huh?" When I told her that I had my undergraduate degree in English Literature and that *Wide Sargasso Sea* was one of my favourite books, she became animated, smiling with pure, childish delight, and telling me about how she'd grown up in Prague, where she'd found *Chronicles of Avonlea* by Lucy Maud Montgomery. The book was in her grand-mother's house, and she'd become hooked on reading, writing, ro-mance, whatever, she'd said, ever since. I could tell by the way she braided her hair loosely over her shoulder, allowing tendrils to fall out and roam around her neck, that she meant it.

Cynthia seemed to have some wonderfully soft parts, and she didn't feel the need to hide them. She never seemed to worry that having sensi-tivities or an imaginative streak could be confused with being weak. It could have been that she was just selective about what she let in and allowed out. I don't know; I didn't stick around long enough to figure it out, but I admired that quality in her: her ability to be two things at once, with one thing never undermining the other.

Cynthia turned her back to me and wiped down the counter with a cloth. It was already clean. I had cleaned the whole kitchen around 3 a.m., scrubbing everything with bleach until the whole area smelled like a swimming pool. This was what one of the army guys who came in said to his friend. I'd retreated to the corner behind the cut-out of Rocky and hid until they left the common area with a couple of the girls. He'd been right. It reeked of chlorine. My nostrils stung.

At the sink, Cynthia rinsed out the cloth. The veins in her arms bulged as she rung it dry. I reached into my bag at the foot of the couch, cringed inwardly as my fingers brushed what I knew was an empty shoulder of vodka, and turned on my phone. I'd turned my cell on and off hundreds of times, hoping my ex would call, hoping he wouldn't.

"So." I looked up to see Cynthia staring at me. "Last night," she repeated. "How was it?"

I looked back down at my phone. "It was all right."

No messages. There were pebbles in my veins, and a tumbling, sinking feeling in my stomach.

"Huh?" Cynthia said.

"I said it was okay."

"So no one then."

I nod my head. Not one.

———→ One of the first things Cynthia had told me was that no girl had to do anything she didn't want to do. ("A couple regulars have a foot-fetish," she said, "but most of the girls here don't want no one touching their fucking feet.") She also said protection was a must. "Condoms all the time. No exceptions. Ever. Even for oral sex. Use them. Don't let them go down on you."

"I let one guy eat me out," Porsche told me later. "I just put some cellophane over my pussy and let him go to town. He has a wife, so I figure he's gotta be a pretty good guy. You know, like, pretty clean." She shrugged and I shrugged too—a baffled reflex to her logic. "Of course, I make him pay extra for it."

Cynthia also told me that no one was under any obligation to discuss their earnings. Each girl was free to decide her own prices and adjust them as she saw fit. As long as she slipped $40 under Cynthia's office door for use of a room, no questions were asked. During the night I was there, I never heard any of the girls talk about the money or the men. They'd lead a guy down the dark hall to one of the rooms and then, usually just a few minutes later, they'd lead him out.

In between clients, they'd sit around the lounge in their various states of undress. One, in pastel lingerie. Another girl, with long, perfectly manicured dreads, wore a white lace bodysuit. Another carried off the Daisy Duke look with incredible precision. I wore yoga pants and a silk camisole. I knew I wasn't going to attract many, if any, clients dressed like this, especially when stacked up against the other girls. That was also the point. I wasn't sure I really wanted to attract anyone.

I wouldn't have admitted that, though. When, before leaving for the evening, Porsche had questioned me about my clothing choice, I'd repeated what Cynthia had told me.

"Confidence sells. Wear what makes you feel good."

What makes you feel fuckable, was what she really meant, which was why Porsche just said: "Uh huh, right." Then left. Which was also why Cynthia was now standing in the kitchen doorway staring at me. One of her arms was propped against the frame, and her hips jutted forward.

She was likely over forty, but something about her stance made me think of a haughty schoolgirl. For a moment, she held my gaze, unblinking, and then sighed, dropping her arm. "Okay. Well, morning kiddo. Grab me a coffee before you come back this evening. None of that Splenda shit. *Real* sugar."

———+ It was a Saturday, so I didn't have to go to my day job. I went back to my apartment and got dressed for a run. I still felt lousy, but I needed to run off the nervous energy and the grungy film of guilt. Tying up my laces, I wondered briefly if anyone who saw me on the street would be able to guess where I'd come from, what I'd been doing or intended to do at some point. As I ran, did I emit a bordello musk? A crimson aura? Did I look, I wondered, like I could be a prostitute?

———+ I was six years old the first time I saw a prostitute. It was 1987 and I was in Pat Pong—Bangkok's night market and red-light district—with my family. My father was still travelling for work and had decided to take us with him.

The air was warm and smelt like fried food and high tide, even though there was no water nearby. My mom had always been a bold traveller, never shrinking from trying new food or venturing out on her own, but that night she was nervous, even though she was trying to exude an air of confidence. You have to be fearless in these places, my dad had explained, or people will try to take advantage you. But my mom was tense. A few moments before, we had almost lost my younger brother after he'd fallen slightly behind. When my mom realized he wasn't with us, she turned around to see him a metre or so away. A man had one hand over my brother's eyes, and the other around his chest, and was backing him out of the crowd. My mother walked up to the man, a tight, rubber band smile stretched across her face. She took my brother's hand and walked away. She hadn't wanted to alarm my brother, or the man, she told my brothers and me years later. She tried to appear calm and even friendly. But she had been terrified, she said. She'd never been so terrified in her life.

The rest of that night, Mom had us maintain an even closer proximity to her, my younger brother holding her hand, and my older brother and I only permitted to circle her in tight satellite orbits. My dad was busy haggling with market vendors for scarves, jean jackets, and hats. My brothers and I made our way through the packed, narrow street, delighted and a little scared. In one stall, there was an ape with a hatchet, cutting off turtles' heads. The woman manning this booth held a cobra by the throat, its tail thrashing wildly. She was trying to convince my mother to let me try a drink. Turtle blood mixed with a little bit of cobra venom. A delicacy, she'd said. It was good for the complexion and would make a beautiful girl even more beautiful.

My mom shook her head but thanked the woman before we moved on. The crowd intensified while the number of vendor stalls dwindled. And the people—they were mainly men. My dad nudged my mother and pointed to a young girl sitting on the lap of much older man outside a bar. My mother looked, her face impassive, but she'd pulled me in closer to her. The girl's hair hung long and limp. Her lipstick was liquorice red and she was wearing a white bathing suit.

I was holding a box. Packed in cotton inside were a tarantula and a scorpion, both dead, pumped full of formaldehyde. Their glossy black bodies were perfectly still and this scared the hell out of me. But from the moment I'd seen them, I'd wanted them.

The man was whispering something in the girl's ear. She smiled into her shoulder and wiggled around like a kitten. I remember thinking she was lovely.

Desire is a funny thing.

"And," Porsche had said, "it's different for women. Women want to be wanted. Men want to want."

It's a funny thing.

———→ Girls. That's what Cynthia called them; and it's what they called each other. The girls, my girls, us girls. Girls, girls, girls. I've tried to stop thinking of them that way, but it stuck. This collective noun speaks of stalled lives. I understand that.

It didn't occur to me then that it was alright to live in the space between states that are precisely defined. I felt trapped by the uncertainty, which I'd grown up thinking was synonymous with weakness. You were one thing or the other. There was no grey area.

Good girls were supposed to graduate from university and be prepared for life. I wasn't. Good girls were supposed to live with their parents until they were married. I hadn't. Yet I did love my parents. I wasn't supposed to sleep with anyone before marriage, but I did. Yet I wasn't a whore. I hated the word and all it implied. Its sound: the weighted start of the word, and the subjugation of its breathy end syllable. I even hated it when the girls called themselves whores; they were beautiful, complex people. Some of them were trying their best, and some were not trying at all, but I didn't think less of them, either way.

———→ I thought less of myself though. I wasn't anything completely, and I felt suffocated by the space around me. I try to pinpoint who I was then and feel her slipping away, slinking across the room like a shadow.

I know this: I craved stability, structure, certainty. So feeling broken, broke, and alone, I picked a side—the side I felt closer to. Back then, I thought I felt closer to the whore because I was one. Now, over a decade later, I've learned that for a flesh-and-blood woman set on defining herself on the basis of absolutes, the whore is always going to be closer.

———→ When I was seventeen, I tried out for the spirit squad in high school, and my father was furious. He said that cheerleading was the first stage of prostitution. He said that cheerleaders show too much of their bodies, too much interest in boys, and wear too much make-up.

My dad said that women look beautiful when they are natural, without makeup. He called makeup body filler. My father insisted that I quit the tryouts. I know that I cried about this. I'd thought I might finally be able to blend in. But my father wouldn't speak to me until I promised I wouldn't go back to practice. He also wouldn't speak to my mother, except to scold her on how my transgression into the whore-dom of Western culture was all her fault. His thoughts on beauty and grace, at least with regard to me, were heavy with Islamic assumption and patriarchal disdain. It's desirable to be beautiful, and it's okay to admire beauty, as long as it is done with modesty and proper distance is maintained. Cheerleading was too obvious. It made girls too visible, and girls who were visible had to put up with shit from men. "And you," my father had always said, "shouldn't take shit from anyone."

These are things I think about now. I can marvel now at how much of my life was foreshadowed and shaped by earlier life events, but for the less than 16 hours I was at the service, none of these things occurred to me. I was operating inside a numb astonishment: Yes, it was happening to me, but I also felt disconnected from it all. I can remember fragments of my time at the service in incandescent detail: the smell of vanilla body cream, certain high-pitched hushed conversations between the girls, the way the rug in the common room felt under my feet, soft and vital. But there's just as much time that's completely blank. I've learned that this is a normal response to traumatic situations. You're acutely aware of what's happening to you when it's happening, and you even know there are emotions you should be feeling—such as fear, sadness, shame—but these feelings are like a distant blip on your radar. You are just going through motions, trying to survive from one moment to the next.

⎯⎯⎯ At around 11 p.m., on the night I was at Cynthia's, my ex-boy-friend did call. I'd been sitting on one of the couches in the common area, which were all pretty much ruined from the oily Greek salads the girls ordered in. I was alternating between flipping through *Better*

Homes & Gardens and trying to conjure meaningful images from the shapes left by the stains when my phone rang. I wedged myself between the wall and an end table, and crouched down before I answered it, as if this would prevent him from seeing me, or more precisely, of knowing where I was. One of the girls crossed from the kitchen to the back hall. If she saw me, she didn't acknowledge it.

He had told me he would be in Ottawa, and that he wasn't planning on returning anytime soon. Things were going well and he was settled. Even though I'd wanted him to call, what he said wasn't what I wanted to hear, so I responded with "Okay" to almost everything. Eventually, he said he had to go. I stayed between the wall and the table until my legs went numb and I had to fall forward and lie there until some feeling returned.

This ex-boyfriend once said that I was the most beautiful thing he'd ever seen, and it used to mean everything to me. I let those words circle around in my mind for a bit. I mouthed the word to myself— *beautiful*. I recalled sitting on our kitchen counter, him cupping my face in his hands, and saying: "I mean, *really*. The most beautiful thing."

Before he left, he'd said: "You warned me. You warned me not to get involved with you, remember?"

I'd told him I didn't, which wasn't the truth, but it didn't matter because all I was thinking was that he was leaving, and that he was trying to make it seem like it hadn't been his decision. But it was.

——— Porsche didn't remember the first man she slept with for money. She said she'd come with her mother's queer notions of finding happiness strange except in the arms of strangers. Porsche said she was a trick baby. Cynthia told me this meant that her mother was a prostitute too.

——— After my run, I showered at my apartment. Then, because I didn't want to go back to the service, and I didn't want to sit around alone, I drove to a drugstore just outside the city limits. I walked the aisles for a couple of hours looking at hair colour, smelling perfumes, trying out hand creams and different shades of blush. I made small talk with a lady about whether it was safe to use Polysporin eye drops on her cat. Eventually, I bought metallic blue nail polish, as well as the remover, and headed out.

———→ I drove further and further north. I wasn't thinking that I would never go back to Cynthia's, even though I never did. I was just letting my mind wander over the hundred-foot granite rock faces tattooed with messages like *Neil and Desiree 4-Ever, 1978, JETS,* and *Anthony loves Tracey.* I was just wondering if Anthony still did.

I was thinking about Porsche's smile, her chipped tooth, and how it made me believe in a world that's incomplete and beautiful.

I was thinking I shouldn't take shit from anyone.

———→ Digressions happen all the time when you've been turning left and right, starting, stopping, and merging. You know that you've been functioning, but you have no idea how you got where you are, or how long you've been gone. You operate on instinct. So, there's a chance that my surprise at arriving at the lake where my grandfather's cottage still stood was genuine, but I don't think so. It wasn't a total surprise.

My grandfather had been a calm, generous presence in my life, always offering his quiet encouragement of my youthful intellectual interests by buying me books about whatever I was interested in: comets, art history, ancient Egypt—anything. One of my clearest memories of him is this: He is sitting on the veranda on a cool summer evening. I have my head on his lap and he is stroking my hair.

My mom had always said that I was the only one he'd let this close. She didn't remember her father being that affectionate with her. I'd hugged this reassurance around myself like a blanket. It was almost dark, and the trees were just spiny black outlines against the sky. There were bats darting back and forth like kamikaze paper airplanes, and fireflies blinking their codes in silence at the shore. There was the sound of water lapping, and there, remembered with clarity, was my grandfather's slow, low voice. I could hear him—gravelly, reluctant, as if speech was being pulled from him. He was telling me about how, when he was thirteen, his father charged him with collecting light bulbs from a manufacturer across the city and bringing them to their family's electric store. He was waiting for a streetcar, his arms loaded with the fragile cargo, when the end of World War I was announced. Then he couldn't get on the streetcar, for fear of the bulbs breaking in the riotous celebration, so he walked all the way back to the shop, dodging festivities and clashing bodies on the city streets. It took longer, but the bulbs all arrived in one piece. He was terrified, he said, that the bulbs would break.

"And you'd get in trouble?" I'd asked. "Your father would yell at you?"

"No, no," my grandfather said. "Likely, he wouldn't have said a thing. But he would have been disappointed, and that would have been worse."

When I was thirteen, my grandfather slipped on a patch of ice and froze to death. He'd broken something, or dislocated something and couldn't get up. He was ninety-two years old, and because he stubbornly insisted on living alone year-round in cottage country, no one found him for days. The cottage went to my uncle, his oldest son. I hadn't been back for years.

When I parked my car at the public boat launch on the lake, it was early evening, that tiny eternity where nothing really happens and the world waits. I climbed up on a hatch-back-sized rock overlooking the water. A few kilometres away, out of sight because of the undulating shoreline and tall Jack pines, was my grandfather's cottage. I wondered if anyone was there, but didn't want to drop in to see. I wanted to be near something good, but alone. In the distance, I heard a motorboat, a loon cry swallowing the sky, but could see nothing except the lightly choppy water and dense forest darkening the Crown Land on the opposite shore. I wrapped my arms around my knees and closed my eyes on the bone-deep familiarity of this place, raising my face to the nebulous sun, imagining myself back to the summers I spent on the lake as a child. I envisioned my grandfather in his orchard, my mother reading on the veranda, my father raiding the vegetable garden for cucumbers. I thought of my brothers and cousins running along the path from the cottage through the woods. I floated, an expanding haze between places, everywhere at once.

Jumptrack

IT WAS 3 A.M., and my older brother and I were cramming my clothes into garbage bags. I ran down the stairs, dumped a couple of the bags on the front steps, and fought against my guts, which were kneading over and over again. Outside, the snow had stopped and stars were melting in the sky.

Matthew was on the way. It was December 14th and we'd been married less than 48 hours. I thought it was a mistake: our marriage. I hadn't meant for it to happen.

A few weeks after the birth of my second child, I'd spoken of this to a complete stranger in a bar. I said it like you'd say you never meant to eat the entire cake: There's a sense of guilt, but also a little pride in the thoughtless overindulgence. Like you had no part in the decision whatsoever. But there you have it—cake face.

Back upstairs, I found my brother emptying the back half of the closet—a space filled with old Halloween costumes, a Girl Guide uniform, a long, garnet prom dress. I told him to forget the clothes and to grab my things from the bathroom instead.

Matthew arrived, confused, but alert. I'd woken him up when I called. There was a gap of two weeks between our wedding day and the day the sale of our home finalized, so he was still living at the apartment he shared with a friend, and I was living with my parents. I'd agreed to move back home two years earlier to complete my Master's degree. I made it conditional on one thing: My dad had to stay out of my life.

By then I'd been living away from home for almost seven years. "So," I said, "if I am going to come back now, you've got to let me just go about my business. No questions or prying. No suspicions. No weirdness."

It was a bold request. I was trying to leverage the fact my dad thought he needed to convince me to come back. The truth was, I had no place else to go. I couldn't afford to live on my own while completing my schooling.

But I was trying to play it cool. I'd said: "I mean it, Dad. It can't be like before."

He'd said: "Okay, if you move back home, I promise." And we'd hugged on it. He'd been so relieved to have me back at that point, he would have agreed to just about anything.

Matthew surveyed the scene. My older brother and I had piled my belongings into trash bags, backpacks, suitcases—whatever we could find. They were all over my room. I was being kicked out without notice, so I didn't have boxes. Matthew asked if I was okay, and I let out a shattered laugh. His calm navigating of my reaction made me uncomfortable.

He said: "Maybe you should rest."

"No," I said. "I want out of here."

———— "No" is just a request for more information. This is one of the first things the stranger in the bar said to me. And he hadn't been speaking just to me. He'd been educating the entire bar, responding to the bartender's question as to whether he wanted a menu. Still, I'd wondered if the stranger had recognized my complaisance right away— that I was a pushover, through and through.

I'd never meant to get married, but I let it happen anyway. I did it because I was three months pregnant. I thought that getting married would appease my father, at least a little, and that would make life more bearable for everyone. I didn't do it because I loved my husband, at least not in the way I thought a person is supposed to love someone they wanted to marry. That all-consuming, passionate love—I didn't feel anything remotely close to that. I felt scared. I felt unbearably lonely.

From the moment I became a wife, I felt uneasy about the label. *Wife.* The word is a stiff apron: it has the smell of spit-up, dish soap and shower douche. That's not me. But Matthew asked, and I said yes. It was typical of me; adapting to survive.

"I don't think it's supposed to feel that way," I told the bar stranger.

"Like what?"

"Like I'm mad at myself for something."

"Life isn't a fairy tale," the stranger replied, crunching ice between his teeth.

I was supposed to be at the bookstore. Matthew had dropped me there so I could have an hour alone, doing something I loved: perusing aisles, buying a new book, and settling into one of the big, engulfing bookshop armchairs for a little uninterrupted reading. I'd spent 15 minutes staring dumbly at the shelves before heading to the bar nearby. The books only reminded me of everything I wasn't doing: I wasn't putting my MFA in Creative Writing to work. I wasn't trying to make the world better.

That was the reason I'd wanted to become a writer. As a child, I saw how my most beloved authors, like Frances Hodgson Burnett, Gordon Calman, and Ann M. Martin, would use fiction to transform the way I thought about the world and my place in it. Now I felt as if I had no place, and I had no right to try to teach anyone anything.

At the bar, I'd sat down beside that particular stranger because he seemed the most sensible—in his 70s and perfectly arranged with a trim beard; like someone who was just waiting for his wife to get her hair done and was killing a bit of time.

"She's at the bakery ordering a cake for our grandson's thirteenth birthday," the stranger clarified as we began to chat. I'd said hello right away, throwing myself into a conversation so I wouldn't have to sit there feeling guilty about not being where I should be.

My pregnancy was the reason I was being forced to leave my house that night. My dad had found out. Though my father had refused to come to my wedding, I'd told one of his friends who did come that I was pregnant. My husband and I had been going around to tables, chatting with our guests, and somehow I ended up mentioning it to his friend. I surprised myself. I hadn't intended to say anything, but the news fell out of my mouth. I saw the information set off a spark in his eyes; he was bursting to relay the news to my dad. My mother had wanted me to wait until after my husband and I moved into our new home to tell my father, but I was tired of carrying the secret around with me. I was tired of secrets in general. It was my wedding day. I was pregnant. I was brimming with feelings which I felt I was constantly having to force back. I wanted the truth out.

I just didn't want to tell my dad myself. I already had my fill of paternal judgment—enough for one lifetime. Even so, as I was relating the news to my father's friend in a nervous rush that could have been taken for excitement, I knew what I was doing was wrong. My father deserved to hear about my pregnancy from me, but by the time my wedding day arrived, I was beyond caring much about anything. It's a near universal truth that weddings don't bring out the best in people. There's so much I wish I could do over, and so much I wish I hadn't bothered to do at all.

Outside my bedroom window, Matthew was trying to cram another garbage bag into his trunk. There was a huge whalebone moon pinned to the sky, and it took up too much space. It was making everything too bright.

My brother called me over. He'd opened a drawer full of sequined and backless tops from my clubbing days and wanted instruction.

"Just leave everything in there." I patted my belly and forced a smirk. "It's not likely I'll ever get to wear them again."

He exhaled a short laugh and pulled at a loose thread on his sweater, and this—this startlingly vulnerable sequence—made me feel sorry for him. I patted his back. "Don't worry. It's okay."

I knew that my dad was livid, and that my brother tried to calm him down. I also knew why my brother thought it was best that I left. Our family's behaviour was too well established: No one fights back. We just move around each other. We just hold our breath and go under.

—————◦ Despite the fog I'd been in since my brother woke me up, and despite our frenzied activity, I was aware that I'd been squeezed into insignificance in my own life.

"I've never seen dad this mad before," my brother had explained, hands and voice shaking. "I don't know what he'll do, and I don't want you to be the one to find out. You should leave, now."

It made sense that he was the one to tell me this: that he was the one battling with my dad. In my dad's absence, he'd walked me down the aisle at my wedding. To this day, my dad will say he wasn't invited. Or, he'll say that he didn't come because Matthew didn't ask his permission—although, prior to the wedding, I'd repeatedly explained that this wasn't going to happen. The first time was when Matthew and I announced our engagement to him.

"Who I marry is not up to you," I'd said. "I'm not chattel."

"It's a matter of respect," my dad retorted, snorting out through his nose.

Matt, who'd been sitting silently this whole time, took a breath to speak up, but I spoke first.

"It's archaic!" I spat, knowing my father didn't know what the word meant. I used it because I wanted to remind him that he didn't know everything about everything. "Besides, Dad," I'd added, "I tried that once—getting a guy to ask for your permission."

I'd been briefly engaged once before. I'd met the guy in my second year of university and agreed to marry him just so I had an excuse to never live at home again. I wanted my real life to begin, right then and there, and I thought this young man could make that happen. The relationship failed, as short-sighted solutions to long-term problems tend to do.

"And even though we came to you first," I said, "you still said no after lecturing us for three hours on how he was a loser and I was an idiot."

I'd learned from that experience. This time, I made it clear that my father was welcome to attend, but the wedding was going to happen either way. He wouldn't be coming, he said. He had made up his mind.

In his absence, I'd asked my older brother to walk me down the

aisle. It strikes me as strange now that I'd even indulge this misogynistic tradition, which relates to the transfer of goods, but once my
mother got involved with the planning, the wedding had taken on a
life of its own and it had precious little to do with me. My mother said
that I would need someone to walk me down the aisle, and she suggested my older brother, so I asked him. We'd grown closer since I
moved back home. We had always been close as children—I'd been
close with both of my brothers then, but that intimacy slackened in our
teenage years. My younger brother had embraced the principles of
Islam. He seemed to follow my dad's lead of disapproving of almost
everything I did. I felt that my older brother had distanced himself
from me to spare himself from being seen as bad by association. He
may not have experienced the same level of censure from my father
over his Canadian habits, but he still had his struggles, mostly relating
to his lack of interest in school, and what my father felt was an exces-
sive dependence on friends. But we all loved each other. Even though I
didn't speak to them often when I'd moved away for my undergraduate
studies, love was never in question. It was easy to fall back in synch
with my brothers once I was home again. Because we were all adults, it
was also easier for us to exercise the maturity required to give each
other the space we required to live our own lives.

Even my younger brother, who didn't tend to conceal his disapproval of many of my beliefs and choices, came to my wedding to show
support. Still, he wasn't the one who ended up facing my father's
rage—probably because he hadn't been the one with an active role in
the ceremony. Or maybe it was simply that my older brother was the
one who was awake when my father could no longer contain his anger.
Either way, it was my older brother who'd woken me up; he stood in
front of me, taking hurried breaths, and searching for something to say
to make it all right.

Finally, he said: "I'm sorry, Ducky." It was the childhood nickname I'd been given, after the duckbilled dinosaur from *The Land
Before Time* who talked a lot. "I know this isn't how it should be for
you right after your wedding."

I wasn't upset. I packed up and left like it was something I'd been expecting. My life had never been mine to begin with. My father let me know this when I was a teenager—every time I tried to tell him that it was my life, and that I had a right to make my own decisions. *Your life affects me,* he'd say. *So it's my life.* I keep wanting to add 'too' to the end of that sentence, but that word never passed his lips.

———→ While my husband and I were piling books into pillowcases, I came across a book from my grandfather, my mother's father, the man I'd end up naming my baby after. It was a *National Geographic* book, designed to introduce children to geometry. I sat down and pored over shapes: hexagons, parallelograms, dodecahedrons. I hoped that the certainty of right angles would bring me a little peace, calm me. But I felt nothing. I had the presence of a damp, heavy sheet tossed over a laundry line.

I'm not here if you don't want me to be. Just impose your will on my world.

———→ There was another man sitting at the bar beside the stranger and me. He said: "Believe what you want as much as you'd like, but gravity's just a theory."

The other man had been speaking for a few minutes, maybe longer. I'd been caught up in my thoughts and didn't register him until the bearded stranger said: "You're an annoying little man."

I hadn't realized that the other guy was talking to me until he looked in my direction, and put his hand to his chest and opened his eyes wide and said: "'Scuse me ma'am. Am I annoying you?"

"Of course you are, you little shit. She didn't come in here to be bothered by you."

The new man squared his shoulders. "Most women don't want to be bothered by me. My girlfriend kicked me out of the car on the highway and told me to walk here."

I tried to imagine what the man's girlfriend looked like and could only picture a scuffed pylon.

The man looked in my direction again, tried to focus on my face, and finally settled on my chest.

"Am I bothering you?"

I said: "No."

The first man said: "Piss off, wanker."

"Rob," he said. "My name's Rob."

"Piss off, Rob."

I smiled into my drink. I was finding comfort in the new man's natural chaos, his unkempt hair, tumbling slouch into his beer, voice like ice cracking.

Rob said: "What happened to humour? The world is suffering. Kinda makes me wanna go home and watch Dr. Phil."

———+ Everyone in my family was home that night, but my older brother was the only one who said goodbye. He gave me a hug and apologized again. My mother and younger brother may have been sleeping. My dad was likely fuming in silence; waiting until he heard Matthew and me drive away. I'd been doing my best to move my belongings quietly, but was struggling to carry one of the pillowcases of heavy books. I dropped it in the hall outside my room. The textbooks thudded against the hardwood floor. I sucked in my breath and paused. Silence. I exhaled and started jamming the books back in until Matthew came and took the pillowcase from me, motioning with his head to go back into my room. I didn't. I stood there, frustrated, watching him.

———+ The first time I saw Matthew he was on a treadmill at the gym. I'd worked there as a personal trainer. He'd been running tall, broad shoulders pulled back, eyes forward. I'd thought, *Now there's amazing posture.*

I thought that he made it look easy. My eyes followed him around the facility. Whether he was running or benching or deadlifting, he made working hard look easy. This is what attracted me: his ability to suffer without giving anything away. I didn't trust people who looked like they couldn't suffer.

Less than six months later I was pregnant. When I'd called to tell him, he'd paused for only a fraction of a second, and then blurted out: "That's fantastic!"

I'd crumbled, sobbing into the phone: "No, it's not."

"Kitty," he'd said, laughing, showing already who would be the more laid-back parent. "Kitty, of course it is."

───→ I pivoted my barstool to face the bearded stranger. "My husband says he knows he loves me more than I love him, and that he's okay with that."

The man sat up straight and rolled his shoulders back. "I've been married for 43 years and I've learned one thing: In every healthy relationship there needs to be a flower and a gardener. The flower needs the gardener to live. The gardener needs the flower so they can nurture it. You can't have two of both. It just doesn't work."

"So what you're saying is—"

"What I'm saying is that you sound like a spoiled flower."

I finished my drink, and ordered another, and then another. My husband called to say he'd be coming to be picking me up soon. I'd asked him to come by and get me at that exact time, but I was annoyed anyway. Another dude intent on ruining my buzz, I was thinking. I texted him that I was at the bar, not the bookstore, telling myself that I didn't care what he thought.

The stranger said: "Don't do that." He was nodding at my drink. My third.

"Do what?"

Another dude stealing my thunder.

"Act like it's all as impersonal as bird shit on your windshield."

I stared him down and finished the entire drink in one gulp. I smacked my lips. "Ah," I said, "like mother's milk."

The man snorted. "You've probably drank more of it."

───→ I had to leave many of my belongings when I left my parents. I shut the door behind me, stepping out of the dead-weight hum of the house and into the car beside Matthew. He squeezed my hand. I reminded myself to let him hold it. He was here, and what I was feeling was not his fault.

That night he tucked me into his bed. He brought a fan into the room and turned it on—a welcome drone. He brought me water and lay beside me stroking my hair. Outside, the snow started again, falling like lemmings.

———• I said goodbye to the stranger. Matthew was waiting in the parking lot with Joe and Nuala.

"I know," I said, sliding into the car. "I know I've kept you waiting."

"It's alright," he said, smiling. I tried to ignore his good nature and turned to the back seat to look at Joe. He was almost two at that time. And Nuala, she was strapped in her car seat beside him. I stroked her tuft of red hair. She was just two months old, and her hair hadn't turned blonde yet.

"They been okay?"

"Perfect."

———• I saw myself sitting in the car—a four-door sedan, kids strapped in car seats in the back, fish crackers strewn all over the floor like confetti. I saw my husband and me in the front—how we must look to the world: one happy family. I chuckled. Matthew looked at me out of the corner of his eye. I rubbed my lips together hard, trying to feel through the numbing tingle of the booze.

But we are happy, aren't we? I wondered. I may have felt my insides being plucked like loose guitar strings whenever I thought of belonging to anyone, or being anyone's anything, but that wasn't our bargain. Matthew and I—we'd never agreed to belong to each other.

> *Love one another, but make not a bond of love:*
> *Let it rather be a moving sea between the shores of your souls.*

———• Those are words from Kahil Gibran's *The Prophet*, read by the officiant at our wedding upon my request. Even then the word love made me prickle: Love. The word had always come with shackles. I balled my hands into fists and tucked them into the sleeves of my coat. Matthew turned up the heat and directed the vents at me. But I didn't feel shackled, not by Matthew, at least, and not by the two tiny people behind me. I felt constrained by what I thought other people expected from me since I'd stepped into the roles of wife and mother. It has always been the myopic stereotypes of who I should be that feel suffocating.

Matthew has never asked me to be anyone; never asked me to be anyone else. I reminded myself of this.

I could see Joseph in my side-view mirror, his mouth slack with sleep and his hat falling low over his eyes. He'd call me mom in his sweet, squeaky voice, and for a moment that would be all I'd want to be for him, forever. But moments like this are breathless, and one can't live without air. No matter who I was trying to be, no matter where, I'd always feel a tug from my navel by some invisible outside force. There was more to life than this.

I don't know if these beliefs are the result of acquired attitudes; perhaps they're the defences I've acquired—a means of never feeling held back, pinned down, and humiliated again. Or they may simply be an intrinsic part of who I am.

We drove home. Chunks of ice were melting in the ditches, and the peacocks from the local farm had wandered onto the road. Matthew got out of the car to shoo them away. One charged and he had to jump to the side. I watched, grinning, imagining their pluck was coming from somewhere in me.

Matthew got back in the car. "Don't think I didn't notice you got a kick out of that."

"No idea what you're talking about."

"Watching your poor, defenceless husband getting attacked by a peacock and laughing."

I replayed the attack in my head and couldn't stop myself from smiling. "Defenceless husband my ass."

Husband or wife. Mother, sister, or daughter. Labels are the armour that keeps us safe; they also keep us too heavy to move. They may have their uses for some, but it's good to strip them off now and then so you can see what you're dealing with. There's an atomic lightness that comes with seeing people and things for what they really are at their root.

At the root of Matthew and me is this: He asked, and I said yes.

Whatever I call him and whatever my reasons were for getting married, Matthew is the only person I want to be around. He's one of the only people I want around me, all the time.

"After all," Rob had said, talking of gravity, "there's gotta be something that keeps your feet on the ground."

Good Breeding

THE WHOLE FAMILY has gathered for Nourouz at my parents' place: It was the same big red-brick house on the Christmas tree farm we'd moved to more than twenty years ago. The only time even half of its rooms were being used anymore was when my brothers and I were over with our significant others and families. It was a lot of space for just two people: five bedrooms, five bathrooms, a den, a library, a living room, dining room, sewing and laundry room, family room, eat-in kitchen, and sprawling rec room in the basement. It was a lot of work to maintain too: a lot of grass to cut, a lot of chasing raccoons out of the eaves; there was trimming, raking, and other upkeep. The house was for sale, and in a matter of months my parents will have moved out.

That Nourouz, we were all sitting around the large golden-oak dining room table. We were drinking tea and digesting a meal of whitefish and *kookoo sabzi*—a verdant and savoury Persian omelette made with spring herbs, barberries, and chives.

While the kids ran off, their fists full of sticky sweet, honey-dipped *Bahmieh* dessert, I was telling everyone a story about a client I had who's half Jamaican and half Japanese. She was a psychology graduate student who needed help editing her dissertation on acculturation and the psyche.

I shouldn't have been relating the story, but I couldn't help it. Being in that house still agitated me. Since arriving a little over an hour ago,

I'd been trying to take comfort in the thought of my own home, 23 minutes away, neat and tidy, but the disastrous aspects of my surroundings were getting the better of me. I couldn't disconnect from it. This was a house I grew up in, and it was an extension of me, still.

"It's interesting stuff," I said, focusing for a moment on the story I'd been recounting. "My client grew up in Japan with her mother, but took after her father's side, physically. It was tough, being so different from the cultural ideal of beauty."

What she'd actually told me was that her cousins teased her mercilessly, and she always felt heavy, silent disapproval from her aunts, who'd exchange their unblinking censure when she'd help herself to seconds, or eat dessert.

"We bonded over our mutual predicaments."

I told myself to stop talking. I knew I was asking for a confrontation, but I felt like the words were being squeezed out of me. The contents of the china cabinets that lined the walls were strewn across the floor: dozens of packages of napkins, broken wax candles in yellowed cellophane, pewter eggcups and brass candlesticks, dusty stacks of plates and serving bowls. Some of them were piled haphazardly, on the brink of toppling.

"What predicament?" my younger brother asked.

"You know," I said, gesturing around me. "Me, growing up in a Muslim household with the wine-slugging White."

The Great White. It's the nickname my brothers and I used for my mom, who is Muslim in name and almost nothing else. She converted to Islam when she married my father, but never declined thereafter to regale anyone who'd listen with tales about her English/Irish/Scottish ancestry. Her maternal grandfather was supposed to sail on the Titanic, but sold his ticket last-minute because his wife was expecting and close to her due date. Her other grandmother had a lowly position but was regal in demeanour as she worked as a scullery maid in the homes of the rich. Her own father's position was that of a respected engineer for Phillips. Her grandfather, George—her namesake—fought in the Boer War. I have two of his bayonets.

Then there were the things she didn't talk about as openly, but shared with me when I was growing up and into my disappointing body. She told me about her childhood nickname, a play on her real name; it had been bestowed on her by the wealthier, more polished girls in her school—Horse-ina.

"Because they thought I was ugly," she'd said. "They thought I looked like a horse."

She showed me pictures of herself as a child. I recognized myself in the chubby density of her body, made more compact by hunched shoulders, lowered eyes. I saw her gap-toothed smile. I saw her hair, a light, velvety brown colour, like the colour of a favourite teddy bear. I saw the blue-grey eyes I've known all my life. I saw my mother, and my young heart broke for her. For myself. There was no hope, was there? We would always carry the insult of our bodies.

Horse-ina. Now, *The White*. She usually bears the title with a combination of amusement, pride, and exasperation. The White: the purveyor and champion of all things bourgeois Caucasian. Also, a protector of all she holds dear. She'd tried to protect me: from the world outside, from my dad's assumptions about who I was; who I'd turn out to be. It's a realization I've come to since having kids of my own: even when my mother told me that I hadn't inherited genes for a commercially beautiful body, she was trying to protect me from my own expectations. You can only do so much.

She'd tried to protect me, but I wasn't protecting her. *The wine-slugging White*, I'd said. Her drinking was a point of contention between her and my father. It hadn't always been. While my father was Muslim, he'd also been raised in Iran during the Shah's rule, and had a more liberal attitude toward alcohol, though he did not drink himself. My mother's drinking became a problem because she was turning to it to deal with her untreated depression and anxiety. As far as we could tell, she wasn't drinking much, but, as I'd learned through my own experience, when you have a mental illness, it doesn't take much for alcohol to affect you badly. It was that, and she was getting older. An older body is less willing to deal with the indulgences of youth: late nights, early mornings, caffeine, alcohol, drugs of any sort. I'd noticed a marked difference between how a hangover felt at twenty-five, and how one felt at thirty-five. My mother was in her early sixties.

Because I'd stopped drinking a few months before, my family

turned to me for help curbing my mother's drinking. They wanted me to help her the way I'd helped myself. I wasn't sure I could. I'd stopped drinking because my mental health had deteriorated so much that I was prepared to kill myself. I had it set in motion: the vodka, the Ativan, the kids at school or with grandparents, my husband at work. I'd been lying on the couch, walking myself through the steps in my head, thinking impassively of my children and feeling relieved. I'd felt lighter and more hopeful than I'd felt since I was very young. That's what had eventually got through to me: if I was feeling something good, even if it was about death, then maybe, I realized, I should give myself one more chance. I would give myself one year precisely. I'd stop drinking and start making a serious effort at taking care of my mental health for 365 days, and if, at that point, life was still shit and I wanted to drink again, I would, or I could kill myself. Or both. I could do anything I wanted, after one year.

I was four months into that year now.

I reminded my brothers and dad of this when they asked how we should go about getting my mother to stop using alcohol as a coping mechanism. How, they wanted to know, had I stopped? I shrugged and quoted John DeVore's essay about quitting drinking:

"There comes a time in every person's life where they put on pants or they don't."

They'd looked at me quizzically.

What I meant was we could be there to support her, but my mother needed to find her own way.

"Jesus," I quoted again, "isn't everyone's Jesus."

If my brothers and father had been looking for me to give them a plan, they were out of luck. For one thing, I didn't consider myself someone who doesn't drink. I was someone who could choose to drink at any time, but was right now opting not to. I needed my options open, I told them. At all times. I'd reminded them that I was the one who asked Matthew to have a vasectomy after Nuala was born, and sent him back for a reversal when I changed my mind six months later. I can't feel trapped by decisions, even if they are my own.

Besides, I didn't feel that I was the person to start giving advice to anyone on quitting drinking. I didn't have a soapbox to stand on. Before, at family gatherings like this, my mother and I would sneak each other glasses of wine and quaff them away from the judgmental stares of my father and brothers. They'd forced us to do it, we reasoned. If they'd just let us enjoy a drink in front of them without being critical, we wouldn't be sneaking them in. What was also true was that they wouldn't have been critical if our drinking hadn't become problematic. The hiding wasn't healthy, and neither was the criticism. But which came first?

Neither. Both.

Intolerance—of our own weaknesses as well as the shortcomings of others: This does the most harm.

My mother and I both had mental baggage we needed to check. Our family needed to help us with it instead of judging us for not being able to carry it.

"Life is a collection of wounds and every wound is thirsty." DeVore again.

Yet there I was, passing judgment on my mother. I dressed it up as a joke, but it was criticism nonetheless.

My brothers were still laughing and I felt my cheeks starting to burn. I met my mother's gaze. There was no sentiment there: no anger or annoyance, just an expanse of silvery spider webs.

I'd begun to wonder how much I really knew about her. As a child, I thought I knew my mother totally, just as all children think they know their mothers completely; by their scent, the feel of their skin, and their solid, unseen presence behind you as you run forward.

At some point, however, I realized that I didn't know much about my mother as a person. I wasn't sure what she really thought, or how she really felt about her life, or about me.

"Okay, guys," I said, looking at the floor, and running my bare feet through the rice Roo had spilled on the carpet. "That's enough. I shouldn't have said that."

"Oh, relax," my older brother said. "She's not as indignant as she looks. She's just white!"

More laughter from the boys—raucous and loud. It sounded like everyone at the table was laughing, but they weren't. My older brother's fiancée wore a strained, pleasant expression, and stared at her fingers, which were wrapped around her glass teacup. My younger brother's wife had turned her attention to entertaining Nuala with Snapchat. My husband was looking out the dining room window, and my father was rolling a dinner napkin into a tight bundle.

I leaned toward my mom and gave her arm a squeeze. She smelled of L'Air du Temps, garlic, and wine.

"Remember," I said to my brothers, "we have white in us too. If Mom really is the Messiah of whites, then we're probably whiter than most purely white people."

Mom smiled. It was a limp gesture, made with only one side of her mouth.

"Anyway," I said, "we're off topic. My point was about how getting conflicting messages about one's identity can mess a person up."

My mom's eyes cleared briefly, and she cleared her throat. "Before your father and I were married, the minister warned me that mixed-race marriages seldom work." She does this a lot: comes into a conversation like a rider cresting a hill; you usually don't know exactly where the rider came from, or where they're going. But in this case, the story was one we'd heard before—often after my parents had a fight.

"I thought he was old-fashioned," she said, "but he was probably right about us."

Because we'd moved into this house when we were approaching adolescence—the time my father felt we were most at risk of being led astray, most of the arguing took place between these walls. There'd been shouting up the winding banister staircase, and then later, when my father installed a P.A. system to enhance the scope and volume of his reach, there'd been explosions over the intercom.

Even now, while volunteering at my children's school, I jump at the sound of the P.A., that buckshot crackle signalling announcements. At my house, when I was growing up, it had usually signalled war. A parent's voice would boom out, demanding that one of us, or all of us, or a certain combination of us, had to get downstairs or upstairs or outside or somewhere *right now*, because, for reasons we didn't yet know, the shit had hit the fan and we were about to catch it. That static snap. What had I done this time?

Back then it used to be my father who was most often upset. These days it has been my mother. They'd be fighting because my dad had left a jar of honey on the counter, or misplaced a teaspoon from the set, or left his mail scattered across the kitchen table. Given the nature of their life together, my mother's feelings of anger at my father are understandable, but because of the way she has chosen to express them—for example, about tidiness, when she herself has all but stopped being tidy in recent years, it's hard to feel the compassion for her I know I should. They knew that the house needed to be market-ready in a few weeks, but there were rooms you couldn't have shouldered your way into. Clothes, boxes, and memorabilia from beloved and deceased relatives barricaded the space, rendering it useless. There was a neglect so great that I couldn't clench my fist against it.

My mom had given up. This is what she said whenever someone came over and saw the mess. "I've given up." Her voice, stance, her whole demeanour was defiant. "I'm tired of cleaning up after everyone."

These days it's become worse than it's ever been. Buried in the back of the laundry room, I found bolts of fabric, reeking of cat urine. The cats have been dead for two years.

My dad has blamed the mess on my mom entirely. My brothers and I blamed it on my mom, mostly. It's been easy to do. After all, my dad's always been a slob, but my mom has changed, and change is not something children easily permit their mothers. The other day I'd decided to go on a bike ride, and because my children had never seen me on a bike before, they'd stood at the picture window of our house, crying and banging on the glass as they watched me go. I was not allowed to step out of their carefully created and precious notions of who they thought I should be.

My mother smoothed the tablecloth with her hands. It was brilliant white, spotless, except where my children had been sitting. Mom would do this: She'd pick one thing and clean it thoroughly: an end table, the kitchen desk, a silver tea set. They'd sparkle.

It wouldn't distract from the mess, though. It would enhance it.

But I wouldn't know whether my mother was trying to distract anyone from anything. Maybe she was trying to clean up—really this time— and would lose momentum. This could happen to anyone—maybe not with cleaning, but with something else. You could be trying to make changes, but get so caught under the heft of your own life, that you couldn't will yourself to budge. Not an inch.

I observed my mother picking a few pieces of rice off the table and putting them on her plate. Her grey hair, the colour of a rain cloud, fell in her face. I fought it down—my dust-choked heart—it was going to disintegrate. Grey: the colour of guilt.

It was difficult to reconcile this woman sitting with us at the dining room table with the mom I'd known growing up. There were few similarities. She used to be so engaged—with her home, with her life. I was trying to accept that she'd become this person not out of apathy or laziness on her part, but out of circumstance and for the sake of self-preservation.

The constant turbulence of her relationship with my father, the stress of running a business, a family history of mental illness, and a laissez-faire relationship with her own prescribed treatments for anxiety and depression—all of it had conspired to create the person in front of me.

And then there was all that stuff about which I knew nothing: her life before me—the things that had happened behind closed doors. I couldn't pretend to know, either, exactly why and when or how my mother became the person I was seeing. I just knew she'd shut down. She'd buried parts of herself. The person left would lash out about things that didn't really matter.

She hit so close to home. I saw myself in the way she bit her lips when she'd tried to put her thoughts together and couldn't. The way she tried to arrange the world around her for protection was familiar. Her hoarding, my compulsive cleaning—they're both obsessive disorders. Hoarding can be a result of OCD, too, even though popular culture would have you believe that people with OCD are always fastidiously neat and organized. OCD is a disease with a diagnosis that gets thrown around with ignorant abandon:

I just have to make sure my counter-top is spotless before I go to work. I'm so OCD!
I have all my spices organized alphabetically. I have OCD!
I have to make my bed every morning with military corners. I know, right? OCD!

—— I have to swallow hot anger when I hear these comments. My disease has taken over my life. It's made it so I've considered taking my own life rather than live for one more moment in my own head. And when I wasn't actively thinking about killing myself, I was passively trying to kill myself by drinking and using prescribed pharmaceuticals.

Obsessive compulsive disorder is not a personality quirk. It's an entire, gawking, maddening mindset. Increasing dialogue to create more knowledge about mental illness is great. Casual appropriation of these illnesses is not. At best, armchair expertise further perpetuates misconceptions about the nature of mental diseases; at worst, ignorance detracts devastatingly from the seriousness of what it's like to actually suffer.

My father, who'd been quiet up to this point in the conversation, suddenly stops twisting napkins and blurts out: "What are you talking about: 'We bonded over our predicaments'? I never told you to lose weight. Maybe I told you that you're too skinny. Women should be *theecker*."

He's obviously missed the point, but I just sigh. "Yes, I know, Dad."

I regret starting the conversation. I slouch back into my chair, folding my arms in front of my stomach to hide the folds of fat. I squeeze and unsqueeze the flesh, five times. It's always an odd number. Even numbers are flawed in their neat divisibility, and if I stop counting on 2, 4, 6, 8 or 10, I'll be condemned to that easily reducible existence for the rest of my life.

Having OCD means that I'll perform repetitive and ritualistic behaviours even though I realize the behaviours are irrational. And even though the way I think and act infuriates me, I can't stop it. I need to complete certain behaviours so my brain clicks. The clicks keep the beast at bay.

My mother's hands shook slightly as she picked up her water glass. She took a small sip and a little spilled onto her chin. I handed my mom a napkin, and she took it without looking at me. I'm a good daughter. I'd tell myself this many times over the next few months. The process of moving my parents would be challenging. My mother would be so difficult and unwavering that I'd consider making an armchair diagnosis of my own: OCPD. Obsessive compulsive personality disorder. My mother, I'd think, has it.

Unlike OCD, OCPD is a personality disorder. This means that people who have it don't think there is anything wrong with their behaviour: It's who they are. Someone with OCPD believes wholly in the purposefulness of their irrational actions. They will aim to control their environment at the expense of being open to new experiences; so when, for example, you suggest to this person that they should throw out hundreds of rodent-nibbled paper doilies that have been crushed into the back of a closet for decades, they will become irate. Indignant. They insist that they're saving those doilies for an occasion your puny brain cannot comprehend. Someone with OCPD will do what they are convinced is right until they push away everyone in their life, and they won't care. There's no flexibility. They are right, and everyone else is wrong.

Many of these character traits fit my mother. Many of these traits can fit just about anyone at a given time—but this is not her. I knew that. Still, in the throes of cleaning, decluttering, packing and moving, it would sometimes be tempting to shove her into a little corner so I could tidy her up. So I could tidy up the way I feel about her.

I'm a good daughter.

We all shatter differently, breaking away over time or all at once. The anger, pity, love, concern, I feel—the mourning—it's not uncommon. We disassemble our parents into pieces we can accept. We all disassemble each other.

I looked around the table. The spring equinox was that day, and the sun had sepia-stained the dining room. Everyone looked like they'd been dipped in silver iodide—dimmed by decades. My younger brother broke the silence at the table. "We weren't raised Muslim."

"What?"

"You said we were raised in a Muslim household," my younger brother said. "It wasn't. It was Dad's idea of Islam. Not real Islam." He was reprimanding me. While he didn't consider himself Muslim anymore, he did consider himself knowledgeable about it. Or more than me. And as the only one of us kids who'd actually been a practicing Muslim at some point in his life, he doubtlessly was. But he was not an expert on my experience of my life.

"Well, as far as I knew," I said, "and based on the way everyone else acted, Dad's word was gospel, and he said we were being raised Islamic, so it was to me."

And whatever it was sucked.

Everyone was quiet again for a moment—long enough for us to hear Roo yelling for my dad from the family room, over the sound of the TV.

"Poppy!" she called.

"And I don't care what you guys say, because you are boys and could've opened a brothel in your bedrooms and Dad would've bought you satin sheets."

I was going to burn through the chair. I knew that I should shut up, but once again, I couldn't because I wasn't making this shit up. When we were in Pat Pong, my dad had said he wanted to take my brothers into the brothels to see the girls. They were both under ten years old, and my mother refused. I don't know if my dad was serious, but the point is this: there was a double standard.

"Poppy!" Roo screamed again, her tiny voice squeaking under the strain to be acknowledged.

"All I'm saying," my brother said, "is that it wasn't Islam."

"I *know* that. Of course I know that now. A lot of it was cultural, or just total Dad-ism and not strictly religious or cultural, but you don't know that as a kid. Dad said we were being raised Muslim. You trust your parents implicitly."

Late afternoon light bounced off the few remaining crystal wine glasses in the china cabinets, shattering the walls. I smelled Roo before I saw her. She'd come into the dining room with a diaper and wipes. She pointed to her bum.

My older brother tried to lighten the mood by pretending to gag. While Roo would always approach her father or me to change her at home, she seemed to think the honour fell to a grandparent when we were at their house. My dad would play with them until he'd be so tired he'd have to crawl up the stairs to bed at the end of the day, but he wouldn't do diapers. That didn't stop Roo from asking. She loved my mom, and worshiped my father.

"Poopy, Poppy."

"Nana," my dad said, chuckling, "that's your job."

"Poopy!" Roo insisted again, scrunching up her face at my dad and squirming around in her pants.

"The Great Calling of the Great White," my older brother teased, and was joined in more subdued laughter by my younger. I straightened my spoon beside my plate.

"You're all idiots," my mom said, pushing her chair back to get up.

There would be a two-month gap between the closing of this house and when they'd be able to move into their new place, a smaller bungalow 25 minutes north of me. During that time, we decided, my mother would live with me, and my father would live with friends. My mom was wary about the arrangement, afraid she'd be in the way in our small bungalow.

"Don't worry," I'd said, patting her hand. "If you can't fit in with your family, there isn't much hope for you anywhere, is there?"

"POOPY!" Roo shrieked.

My husband, who'd been sitting in tactful silence for most of the meal, got up.

"I've got this." He whipped Roo up under his arm, inciting peels of giggles from her, and dusting us all with a whiff of infant crap.

"Thank you," my mom sighed, brushing her hair off her forehead. "It's nice to know someone here has good breeding."

The Cosmic Script

I'M WIDE AWAKE, eyes open to absolute darkness. Someone is in the room. They've just come in. I know this even though I can't see or hear them. The fan beside my bed hums. My skin is tingling. I feel the weight of the room shift, an unseen, uneasy energy. I hear a sniffle.

"Nuala?" I ask.

"Yes, mommy."

The room tilts back to centre.

"Jesus. What are you doing?"

"Can I cuddle you?"

I lift the sheets up and scooch back. "Come on, then." She scurries under the covers, burrowing into my body. I wrap my arms around her. She smells like crayon wax; the soft skin on her thin arms feels painfully vulnerable. I bring her in a little closer, pushing the hair back off her forehead. I close my eyes. Then her small voice comes to me from beneath the mass of sheets.

"I'm going to die, aren't I?"

My eyes open. I try to focus in the darkness. It takes me a moment to respond.

"Why are you thinking about that?"

I feel her shrug. I can picture her small shoulders, the curve of her clavicle to scapula—that elegant attachment.

"Bad dream?"

Another shrug. I stroke her hair slowly, trying to piece together words. I stare forward, eyes flooded with nothingness. My room is pitch black, a recommendation from my doctor to help improve my sleep hygiene. "Sleep hygiene" is how he described it, and the tidy summation of good sleep practices appealed to me. Sleep in complete darkness. Sleep in a cool, bordering on cold, room. A temperature of 67 degrees F is ideal. No electronics in the bedroom. I lowered the temperature, banished cell phones, bought blackout curtains, and sleep in a darkness so saturated that I can't see my hand in front of my face.

Nuala turns so she's facing me, hugging one of her legs around my waist and nuzzling her head against my chest.

"No, no dream, Mommy." She pauses. "Just woke up and knew."

On the eve of my tenth birthday, I'd woken up just before midnight. There was no reason I could fathom. I was just awake, staring at moonlight slipping in from behind the roller shade. It hit me: the next day I would go from being 9 to 10 years old. I was entering the double digits, and chances were, I knew, I'd never get out. I would be 10, and closer to dying than ever.

Years later, I'd learned that fear of death is a common preoccupation for people with OCD. It makes sense. Out of all the things in life that are beyond our control, death is the most inevitable. The prospect of one's own demise is terrifying for most. For someone with OCD, whose anxiety is already heightened, it's debilitating. From the time I could first grasp the certainty of death, which for me was around age four, I'd been consumed by it. Not in any fleeting way, where I could passively acknowledge that, yes, I am going to die, but in a bowel-quickening sense. From a very young age, I knew—I really understood—death was coming. For me, and the people I loved. And there was nothing I could do about it.

I couldn't shake the feeling I'd awoken with on the eve of my tenth birthday for months, and my mother took me to our family doctor. *Talk to him about it*, she'd insisted. Instead, I'd asked him about a series of lumps that had appeared all over the backs of my legs. Cancer, I'd been certain. *Cellulite*, my doctor had said.

I didn't talk to him about my anxieties that day, but I would a few years later, when these bouts of obsession with mortality got longer and harder to shake. The realization that I was going to die continued to haunt me, as fresh and terrifying as it had ever been.

Nuala sticks her hand into my armpit, a habit from when she was a nursing baby. She turned six a few months ago.

"Honey, it helps if I know why you're thinking about this."

"Why?" she says. "Is knowing that going to stop me from dying?"

I sigh.

Last year, she had to be removed from the school Jump Rope for Heart assembly. The video they'd watched showed images of sick children and adults, and while the message was one of hope and rising above adversity, that's not what Nuala saw. She saw the other side of this optimism, and she'd been inconsolable. This year, her teacher has assured me she will be excused from the assembly altogether.

Nuala's body is knotted with tension. I stroke her hair.

"Nuala," I say, trying to keep my voice calm and soothing. "I'm just trying to help."

I'm just trying not to say, yes, you are going to die and there is nothing I can say or do to change that.

We don't know for sure whether Nuala has OCD. Her doctor says it's possible, even likely, that Nuala has inherited some form of anxiety disorder, given her behaviour and the family's history: my own and my mother's, and those of my aunts and uncles, great aunts and uncles, and grandparents. Most experts agree that mental health issues run in families and that every family has some history of mental health problems. What experts don't know exactly is what part of these disorders originates in our genetics, and what part is the result of our experience. Nurture vs. nature—that old chestnut. It seems impossible to tell. It will likely remain impossible to tell, if you want a pat answer across the board.

Everything bleeds—one thing into another. I don't want to burden Nuala with a label right now, and all the shaping and misshaping that goes with it. So other than checking in with our family doctor, I have not solicited another opinion. What I do is try to monitor Nuala's anxieties. I encourage open conversation. I always listen. I never make her feel that what she's saying and feeling is inconsequential or abnormal.

"It's completely normal to have these feelings," I tell her. I say: "You're so smart and brave, do you know that? So many kids—so many people—don't have the guts to even let their brains think about this stuff. That's how big and scary it can seem. But here you are, taking it on, and you're so clever, knowing when you need to talk to someone about it. I'm so glad you're telling me this. That's the best thing you can do, baby. Don't ever bottle that up."

When I first confided in my mother that I had thoughts about death and dying, she told me not to worry about it. We were driving home from a craft show, and I had new barrettes in my hair—white ruffled-lace with delicate blue trim and a small, blue heart-shaped button sewn into the middle. I remember looking out the window, thinking that they matched the clouds, and that's where my mom had said we'd end up when we die. Up there, in heaven.

She'd said: "Even when we die, we'll be together there, eventually." I tried to digest that. I sat in the back seat of our diesel Volvo and looked at the rolling marble sky, the empty fields and the electrical towers that loomed like apocalyptic giants. I tried to picture my mother and me in heaven together, enjoying some radiant, diaphanous existence, and while her words offered temporary relief from the anxiety by giving me something else to hope for, it would always come back to this: I didn't believe her.

I'd asked my father and got a similar story. Don't worry. There's a heaven and a God and a prophet, Muhammad, who will make sure all good people are rewarded with a place in heaven.

I'd asked a serious question, and had been given a pat on the head and a whole lot of pap. I realize now that many children accept these stories as truth. I don't know what the difference is between me and them. Maybe they had parents who took them to houses of worship, so the stories had real, tangible meaning in their lives. Mine didn't. My father prayed twice a day, but no one else did. We didn't attend mosque, either. God. Heaven. Hell. Muhammad. These were people and places out of fairy tales, like dragons, mermaids, and enchanted forests. I wanted to believe they existed, but ultimately, I didn't. And because I didn't believe when everyone else seemed to, I knew there was something wrong with me.

Don't worry. Those words. I've been critical of my parents' use of them for most of my life. I couldn't *not* worry, and my fear kept going around and around in my head, gaining traction, unravelling their stories.

As critical as I've been though, I've had to fight down saying those exact words to Nuala. I understand now: You say them because you don't know what else to say. You tell the stories about life after death to your children because even if they're not true, they make life more bearable, and you owe them this, at least. You've brought these small beings into the world only to flicker, fade away, and eventually be forgotten.

Your beautiful children.

How could you?

Nuala's been crying, quietly. Her cheeks are wet. My shirt, damp.

"Honey ...," I say.

"I just want this feeling to go away," she whispers.

"I know," I say. I wish I could breathe her in; absorb her back into my body so she'd be safe. There's so much out here to hurt her. There are so many ways she can hurt herself, just trying to make herself feel better for a while.

People who exhibit symptoms of OCD in childhood are more likely to develop a problem with drugs or alcohol—anything to help deal with the incessant anxiety. I tried it all and nothing helped. What did help was meeting a neuroscientist with OCD in a support group a year ago. His life's work centred on finding a way to preserve the life of the brain, forever. I didn't know whether he would actually be able to do this, and the thought of an eternal life for the mind was not what eased my mind. But he'd mentioned something about scientists stumbling on a relatively new organ in the human body.

The interstitium, he'd explained. It lines the digestive tract, among other places, and in current research it may explain how diseases like cancer spread. Scientists used to think that the interstitium was connective tissue.

He was using this fact to illustrate his point about how new discoveries were being made all the time, so his mission to prolong the life of the human brain was completely within the realm of possibility. I was thinking of the discovery in another way: proof that we know absolutely nothing about anything. Everything we think we know can be suddenly overturned.

Nuala says: "Can I turn on the light?"

I reach over her and switch on my bedside reading lamp. Nuala and I squint each other into focus. I rearrange the pillows, propping myself up into a seated position. Nuala crawls into my lap, her long legs folding up to her chest.

"Ugh," I grunt. "You're getting so big."

She looks up into my face.

"Gramps says there's a heaven and a God. Are there?"

My dad, putting ideas into my children's heads. Maybe he assumed I would have already told my kids about heaven and God. Or maybe he didn't think about it at all, and was just answering a question with his truth. Either way, these concepts are pervasive enough that Nuala was bound to ask me about them eventually.

I force myself to push my agitation with my father aside and think of the interstitium.

"I honestly don't know, Nuala." I can feel her small heart beating through the side of her rib cage. "But I think there could be." Maybe not the heaven and God of religious texts, but something else. Some other place we go when we die. Some other kind of prime mover.

"So you don't know?" She pushes herself off my chest and looks directly into my eyes. Her voice is becoming pinched, high. I wish Matthew was home. These days, he's working nights in the city.

I take a deep breath and tuck her hair behind her ear. "No, honey. I don't. Not for sure. But here's what I think. I think we know absolutely nothing about anything."

I tell her about the interstitium, and about the discovery of gravitational waves. I tell her about how the smartest men in the world used to think the earth was the centre of the universe, but that now we know it's not and the universe goes on and on indefinitely. I tell her about long-orbit comets and how they travel through space for millions of years. Who knows where they go. Who knows what they see.

"We have no idea, Nuala, how big it is. How much is out there and how little we know. And if our knowledge is imperfect, then our fears are unfounded." This is the same thing I tell myself, everyday.

Her eyes soften, losing their desperate pleading edge. She puts her head back on my chest, her mass of blonde hair bronzed by the dim light from the lamp. I feel the predictable give of her body into mine.

"We know so little about life, and we're living it. How are we supposed to know anything about death?"

Nuala looks up at me. "It could be anything," she says. "It could even be something really amazing."

Exactly.

"Like how when a mother is pregnant with a baby, that child's cells can move into the mother's body, and stay with her, in her brain, and other parts of her body. This means that even when you are at school or with Gramps or Nana, you are still with me. People didn't know about that before, but now, we do."

Nuala puts her hands on either side of my face and peers into my forehead, as if she is looking at the cells in my brain, little cosmic specks of herself.

"That," Nuala says, "is pretty amazing."

It's strange how you can't see yourself in your children's impossibly clear eyes, but you are all they see. They grew in you, and it didn't happen all at once, but your body's bottomless pitch let out their surging light. It's strange how my children come to me in the night, their small, compact bodies sweating bad dreams; how they relax into my umbilical circumference, and I relax into theirs. It's strange how I'm an endless source of comfort for them and I've never been one for myself.

Vanity Muscle

P AIN IS BEAUTY.

I heard this countless times during the decade I worked as a personal trainer. Pain is beautiful. Picture a woman in her mid-40s seated on the bench of a cable rowing machine. She's incrementally overweight; her sports bra digs into her skin just enough to show that she believes in something outside of herself. She's come to the gym on her lunch break and is hungry and a little lightheaded. She's struggling to pull the handle grip to her ribs, just under her chest. There's sweat trickling from her hair line, which shows the odd strand of grey sprouting in short, wiry exclamations. Picture her gritting her teeth, tensing her jaw, trying to focus on the words of her trainer. He's telling her to engage her core (she doesn't know what that means), and squeeze her shoulder blades together (her arms are going to rip out of their socket, she's sure of it). She sees her reflection in the mirror, since dozens of mirrors line the wall in front of a succession of fitness machines. She's shocked to recognize the snarling face in front of her as her own; her lip has curled, uncontrollably, and her civil-servant smile appears ripped from her face by exertion. She's processing all this and her trainer tells her to push harder because this pain is beauty.

It's the last rep of the last set. The last instant of the last interval. The last push.

She keeps her elbows down, locked into the sides of her body and brings them back as far as she can, pinching her shoulder blades until rip-tide heat tears through her back. She lets go, and the cable snaps the handle forward so it clangs loudly against the footrests of the machine. It *is* beautiful, she thinks—beautiful in the way that pain makes you grateful for its absence when it's over.

I never could bring myself to say those words to any of my clients, but I watched many other trainers use the phrase to motivate theirs. I wondered if it truly resonated. I wondered if it really made more sense to them than it did to me. Even though I accepted the words on a super-ficial level, a deeper part of me recoiled every time this bit of *fitspo* was used. I suspected it was the same part of me that knew I would never be able to suffer enough to be beautiful. So, to avoid confronting this suspicion, I didn't question my unease. I avoided it with side-long glances in the locker room mirror.

Showing pain is weakness—a personal failing. I have enough of those.

———— A maternity room nurse has just finished looking over my contractions. She read them from the cardiotocograph, and is now fid-dling with the heart-rate monitor. The alarm has gone off again. The number 43 flashes back at us and she turns to look at me.

"There's nothing wrong," I explain, lifting myself onto my elbow, exhausted and hazy, but making a point of being extremely polite be-cause I'm also embarrassed. The pain isn't bad yet, but I know it will be, and the prospect of losing my composure is humiliating.

"My heart rate is always like that. It's just the way I am."

The nurse talks over her shoulder while fiddling with the buttons on the monitor. "But this is low. Really low."

"It's normal for me."

The nurse turns and looks me up and down. She adjusts the sensor attached to my finger, and then adjusts the baby's monitor. His heart rate is distant and undeniable, like a herd of galloping horses on the other side of a mountain.

"But it's not even increasing much with contractions. That's unusual."

I shrug. "Not for me."

The nurse raises her eyebrow and turns away again.

Matthew is sitting in a chair in the corner of the room, quietly listening. The whites of his eyes are shot red, the irises, shock blue. We'd been about to have dinner when my water broke and the contractions started. Ten minutes apart. I'd called the hospital and told them I was coming in immediately. With a fourth pregnancy, I knew, things can move fast.

I feel another contraction building, low and strong. The monitor flashes 45.

The nurse says: "Are you *sure* this is normal?"

A second nurse comes in. I'm relieved to see a face I recognize: the nurse who gave me my maternity ward orientation a few weeks ago. She'd sat patiently across the table while I prattled on about wanting pain relief for this delivery.

"I've done natural labour," I'd said, shoving my fingers under my thighs. It was January, and as usual, I was underdressed. I wore ripped jeans and a sweater, that's it—no outerwear of any sort. The missing extra layer of clothing took too much effort to manage; it meant finding hangers for coats and shoving hats and mitts in sleeves and pockets, only to find out when I got home that I'd lost something somewhere, because I'd rushed. I also didn't want to hold someone up or leave someone waiting while I fumbled. It was too cumbersome, too chaotic. I'd rather be cold. "And I've done natural labour multiple times. I've had my moment of wanting to feel connected to my foremothers through the pain of drug-free labour, but I'm over it. I want drugs. *All* the drugs."

The nurse had smiled softly. "We're here to make sure you have a safe, happy experience and a healthy baby," she said. "You don't have to justify yourself, honey."

Yes, I do. Listen. Pain is needy. It doesn't want to be ignored.

The night of my orientation, my head had been throbbing, and I was exhausted from forcing myself up at 5 a.m. to work out when I hadn't been able to get comfortable enough to fall asleep until after midnight. Then, I had a full day with assignments and caring for the kids. I had been hyper, unfocused, and unproductive. I'd spent Roo's naptime reorganizing emails instead of doing actual work or napping myself. And at the orientation, instead of telling the nurse about my OCD and how it will make my staying at the hospital for 24 hours after delivery difficult because I won't be able to work my way through my ticks, I'd instead given in to all the noisy, useless thoughts and ideas tumbling around my brain. I'd tried to focus on the nurse, her microbladed eyebrows, bright pink Sketchers, royal blue scrubs, brown shoulder-length hair that looked soft, too soft to be on an adult.

My hands were still cold but my body felt hot.

When I found out I was pregnant, I'd stopped taking the supplement I'd been using to help control my OCD: N-Acetyl-Cysteine, more commonly known as NAC. The supplement is a form of the essential amino acid cysteine, which is used by the body to produce an antioxidant called glutathione, also known as GSH. There's convincing research that shows GSH can help treat various psychological and mental conditions, like autism and Alzheimer's disease, as well as anxiety disorders—notably, obsessive compulsive disorder.

NAC had been prescribed to me by a naturopathic doctor. I'd sought one out when I was trying to shake my dependence on lorazepam and valium. I'd been to see my doctor about alternatives to these sedatives, but had been presented with other brands of pharmaceuticals. He wasn't convinced I'd fare well off the medications. I wasn't convinced I could fare well on them any longer. Their slow-dissolve, blissed-out appeal was burying me. With every pill, I became more unrecognizable to myself—something I'd wanted almost my whole life, but not in this way. Not as a bloated, dead-eyed, muscle-twitch zombie. I promised my doctor I'd taper off the medication, and I did, at the same time as I started taking the NAC. My naturopath also recommended lavender oil pills to take as needed, to help mellow my mind. They worked almost instantly. It's difficult to say when the NAC took effect. Withdrawal from the medications was slow. I can say that at the end of the three months it took me to get off the pharmaceuticals completely, I felt an old, familiar rawness return. It was spring and the world was so green it hurt. The sky was too wide: too blue. And in the afternoon, the air was so whipped butter soft that it reduced me to tears. All this beauty; it was all going to end. I felt my temporality in the world with this intensity again, but I was bothered less by it. I could breathe through it.

I considered that this ease might be the effect of my realization that suffering is relative: This raw incarnation of pain was more bearable than the alcohol and drug-induced one I'd endured for years. I also considered that my more mellow mood was the work of the NAC completely. Since taking the supplement, I could more easily arrange my thoughts—the ones that are important, those I should listen to, over the ones that I should muscle out.

But I think it was a bit of both.

There's been no proof that taking NAC during pregnancy will harm an unborn child, but there's been no proof that it won't, either. It's unethical to test on pregnant women, my naturopath had explained, so we just don't know. It's best not to take it, if I can manage. And for the most part, I could. Off NAC, I didn't experience the same frantic despair of my preteen and teenage years which caused me to eventually start using substances. Neither did I fall into the black mouth void of that period, but without the supplement taking the edge of the urgency of every thought, I can't deny that it was more difficult to control them.

I'd smiled too widely at the orientation nurse, fanning my face with my hand and taking short, erratic breaths to try to cool my face, my body.

"Can spontaneous combustion really happen?" I was saying. "I mean, I was in this course in university called Medicine and Literature, and we read excerpts from publications like *Philosophical Transactions*. Have you ever read that? It was put out by the Royal Society in London and wasn't confined to papers on medicine. The publication had articles on astronomy, geology, biology—the works. Amazing stuff! Anyway, there were these reports written by doctors on what appeared to be spontaneous combustion, and almost all of the victims were women. They were women of the streets, if you know what I mean. They were heavy drinkers, and all a little on the chunkier side, like me, and they all carried most of their heft in the mid-sections, which is where the combustion seemed to happen. All that fat just ignited or something, and their torsos were almost completely consumed. You could smell the fat sizzling; that's what the reports said. And their arms and legs were untouched and their faces a little singed, but their stomachs"—I open my hands and widen my eyes—"just puddles of lard."

I'd laughed nervously; that automatic, spring-loaded sound.

"If only it were so easy to lose weight, right?"

The nurse had stared at me with her mouth open, her microbladed eyebrows, unmoved.

I shook my head; the sound of loose change shifting in a coin purse. I took a deep breath. "It's just that I want you to understand I've done it—the no pain management thing. I'm not trying to cop out. I've run marathons. I've worked out every day of this pregnancy. I did burpees just this morning."

What I'd meant was: I'm strong. Really, I am.

"Most women use pregnancy as an excuse to lay off their workouts," the nurse had said. "You know, enjoy getting a little baby fat."

"No." I'd looked up, meeting her eyes directly for the first time. "No way."

Fat had always been an affront to my neatly arranged and fragile understanding of the world. There's the messiness of it: all that extra flesh. I wanted to rub it out, tuck it away. This irritation was confounded by the growing number of people who seemed fine with having excess fat. At best, I would dress up my feelings of discomfort as concern for their health. At worst, I'd comment on how obese individuals were a burden on the resources of society and the planet. They ate too much, then needed too much medical care. Even as I made these arguments, I knew I wasn't being honest.

I was angry, sure, but it took me years to understand that I was not angry because these people were overweight. I was angry because by being okay with having extra fat, they were thumbing their noses at a system that I was desperate to be part of. I wanted them to suffer, like me, and their unwillingness to do so was enraging. It implied that I was killing myself for nothing, and had been my whole life.

———→ Pain is lonely.

My mom kept a box of Slim Fast bars in a kitchen cupboard for ten years—from the time I was ten to age twenty. It was the same box with only two bars missing. There was also a container of Slim Fast Shake, chocolate flavoured. She did aerobics classes, off and on, too, and occasionally went for walks. As far as I could tell, she never lost weight.

I used to wish she would.

I knew, early on in life, that my mother fell short of embodying the absolute beauty prized by society. There were beautiful elements to her: high cheek bones, soft, even skin, arching Scarlet O'Hara eyebrows, but she was always a bit too much. Her bottom too flat, hips too wide.

Beautiful women had trim tummies, thin arms and legs, pert backsides. They had long hair. I grew up in the 1980s in North America, and these standards of beauty were everywhere—on TV, in magazines or billboards, and even in my mother's own attempts to reshape her body. Body-positive movements didn't exist. Female physical strength over thinness wasn't celebrated. That would come decades later, but when I was a child, the standards of beauty were pervasive and narrow, and I ruthlessly measured my mother against them.

As I grew up, I ruthlessly measured myself.

My mother also had short hair, which I hated. I wished she'd grow hers long, like one of the gorgeous women on the soaps she watched, but she said she liked it short. It was easier to take care of. She also said my dad liked women with short hair, which was, I suspected, the main reason she kept it cropped and curled. At the time, short hair on women was popular in Iran. I'd see pictures of my relatives and my dad's friends sitting around a large blanket on the floor, eating together, and all the women had short hair. He wanted me to have short hair too, and until I got old enough to insist on what I wanted, it was. After that, my father allowed me to grow it long. It was a small concession in an otherwise strict code regarding what was aesthetically permissible.

I grew up sandwiched between Western and Middle Eastern ideals. While there were some similarities, in terms of how beautiful women wore makeup, had big eyes, smooth skin and ample breasts, there were more differences. Thinness, for example, wasn't as prized in the Middle East. My father was never concerned about my mother or me being a little overweight. *Theeeeker.* This could also have been his personal preference, but I've since learned that wasn't it. The Iranian female singers and actresses of the time were all curves and softness, and this was the ideal there.

Then there was the matter of modesty. In Western culture, the female body is something for everyone to admire. In Middle Eastern culture, it is something only for a husband to admire. In both cultures, the female body is an object. These were the competing strings of discord and harmony, and as I grew up, they dragged me along.

With enough strings you get a rope—a noose. Go ahead and hang yourself.

———— By my mid-twenties, I was a bulimic with an ever-fluctuating BMI, and a dependence on booze and pills to drown out the knowledge that I'd never be enough. I was also not even attempting to manage my OCD, having gone off my medication by my second year of university because I wanted to lose more weight, and the pills I was taking had made it difficult for me to do so. This was also when I'd decided that I eventually wanted to get certified as a personal trainer. I believed that if I could call myself an expert on bodily perfection, then I'd be more likely to finally achieve it. I thought that I'd not only have the knowledge to provide my own back up, but that I'd also be part of a system that would motivate me to look the part of someone who's an authority on physical beauty. I threw myself into it. Over the years, I trained hundreds of clients, as well as myself. I ate little during the day, could recite the caloric value of just about any food, and at night, I drank vodka and water to numb the hunger. I'd wake up hungover and my body would drive me to eat. I'd do so frantically, and guiltily, and then I'd throw it all up after.

I knew that if I kept drinking, I would always be bulimic. I knew that the need to eat fatty foods is a physiological reaction to the shitstorm inflicted on the body by alcohol. I knew that drinking was boosting my levels of galanin, a hormone that increases desire for fats.

I also knew that as humans we're driven to crave fatty foods post-boozing because when we eat high-fat foods our brains produce opioids—those funky, feel-good chemicals that can help mitigate the pain of a hangover. Then there's the way alcohol affects sleep. I knew that drinking doesn't allow people to get proper sleep, which results in an increase of ghrelin, the body's hunger hormone.

The lack of sleep also affects mood, as does alcohol's tendency to mimic serotonin, one of the body's happy hormones. When the body gets serotonin from alcohol, it makes less of its own. This is why people feel miserable when they are hungover: It takes a while to restore chemical balance. And this is why people who have mental disorders are so often advised to avoid drinking; bio-chemically, they already have a volatile hormonal balance, and alcohol throws that further out of whack.

I knew all this, but if you have all the information in the world and you don't use it, it's worthless.

Pain is stupid—a dumb, deaf, mindless thing.

By the time I left personal training, I had two children under two years of age. Late nights, early mornings, overtraining, under-eating, and too much drinking had left me overwhelmed and defeated.

The title of personal trainer hadn't moulded me into the person I wanted to be, with the body I wanted to have. It's sad and a little funny that I'd convinced myself it would.

I've only recently been able to start implementing one of the profession's simpler edicts: the principle of muscle hypotrophy. You tear muscle fibres, then allow them time to grow back stronger.

You rest.

I try. When I first learned I was pregnant with my fourth child, I'd promised myself I'd relax more. During previous pregnancies, I'd fought my body's inevitable expansion with daily workouts, and even though I ate as instructed for pregnant women, I ate no more than absolutely necessary. And this was fine. Most of the time, I loved exercising, not only because it kept me thinner, but because it made me happy. More than happy—it gave me a little taste of invincibility. *This* is what my body can do. *This* is what I'm capable of: my potential unleashed.

But sometimes I'd pushed too hard, too often, and the thought of exercising became exhausting. Squeezing in time for my workout became one more thing I felt I had to do.

So this time, with this pregnancy, I'd told my husband that I was going to really enjoy the coming months. I was going to sit around if I needed to and not feel guilty about it. If I only work out three days a week, I was going to be fine with that. If I wanted to eat cake, I'd eat cake. I was going to relax my expectations.

"Yeah," Matt had said. "Yeah right."

I've worked out more often, and with more intensity in the last few months than during my previous pregnancies. I've needed it more than ever. While I haven't been bulimic for years, I still exhibit disordered eating, a term used to describe a less severe type of eating disorder. I still don't enjoy food. I get tired of having to use it to silence my body's whining hunger. Then there's the fact I'd only been off pharmaceuticals and alcohol-free for less than six months before becoming pregnant. My doctor agreed: He said that I should be careful not to overtrain, but if I needed to lean on exercise more than usual, do it. Do whatever it takes. Compared to my other, more detrimental body-centric obsessions, exercise was harmless.

So when the orientation nurse had told me that most pregnant women use pregnancy as a time to relax, I'd joked.

"I'm too lazy to fight to get my body back. It's easier not to lose it in the first place."

Now, the orientation nurse is waving away the other nurse, the one who'd been concerned about my vitals. "Oh, she's fine. She's in great shape, and has a very healthy heart."

She feels my stomach, checking the baby's position.

"So," she says, ignoring the other nurse, who is standing behind her, still looking at the monitor screen, unconvinced by the assurance that nothing is wrong, "I'm going to change the settings on this monitor, so the alarm doesn't sound every time you relax."

She adjusts the heart beats per minute from 65 to 40. "That look about right?"

I nod and lie back. I should be strong enough to withstand others' judgment on my own, but some days it's too much. With each pregnancy, I've watched my body become part of the public domain. Women are criticized for gaining too much baby weight. Women are criticized for not losing baby weight. When I take steps to avoid having to gain or lose any unnecessary weight, I'm criticized for that too. I feel as though I'll never be able to outrun the judgment, but I can train myself to resist it, to withstand it. That's easier to do with the support of other women.

My orientation nurse leaves, and the remaining one looks over the transcript of my contractions.

"They're getting closer together," she says. "You still want an epidural?"

I look to Matthew. He nods at me, offering encouragement.

"If you want one, I'm going to have to page the anaesthesiologist now."

I'm not the first woman to wish her husband could give birth in her place, but in my case, it's just because I want him to say the word for me. *Yes.*

Another contraction builds, and my ears start to ring. I close my eyes, picture a wave, and try to ride it.

When I open them, the orientation nurse is here again with a man I don't know. "The anaesthesiologist," she explains, helping me sit up and undoing the back of my gown.

"But she didn't say she wanted one," the other nurse says.

The orientation nurse helps me swing my legs off the bed so I face her. The anaesthesiologist moves behind me and starts tapping on my spine. "Put your arms on my shoulders and round out your back," the nurse says. "Yes. Perfect. Now he's just going to see if he can find a good spot, and then you have to sign a form."

I nod. Her hair against my hands is a toddler's—a fistful of nebula.

The other nurse repeats: "But she didn't *say* she wanted one."

Another contraction builds, and my body tenses. The nurse rubs my forearm, running her hand over a constellation of bleached scars. Sometimes pain is just pain. I breathe in, envisioning blood bubbles coming out of my ears and floating up, away. I follow them until they pop, one by one. I exhale slowly.

Somewhere behind me, the other nurse takes a breath, is about to say it again: "But she didn't ..."

"Yes." I look up into the face of the nurse in front of me. She winks and repeats: "Yes, she did."

Pain can be beautiful.

It is beautiful in the way it can eventually create something strong.

Naming Baby

HE HAS MY last name.

He has it because he's mine—my fourth child and a last chance. My name because of his puckish brutality and his milkweed tuffs of hair against my face in the dark.

The luxury of finding familiar skin, so close.

Because my name means power. Because of his first name, given after my uncle, who died at 58 of brain cancer.

My uncle, as a child, ran through the house calling to his mother: *You're very nice, I love you.*

(I love you, too.)

Because of sparkling idolatry; my baby's eyes—they're warm asphalt after the rain.

Because of sticky sweetness that chokes you; a handful of sun-soaked raspberries bleeding sweetness down your throat. Because I say it and it feels like home.

Because I'm lonely.

Because we all need to fatten our ghosts.

He has my last name because I'm the Queen of Warming Up, and it took three kids before it occurred to me to use it. My mental acuity was compromised by illness for so long that I didn't consider the significance of nomenclature; how in naming something, you name your price. You spell out how desperately you long to hold, possess.

Me—someone who wants to belong to no one.

Because it took three kids for me to conceive of a connection to them. Before, I'd done what came naturally: I'd buckled. I gave my first three kids their father's last name, which is a point of intersection between both of the cultures to which I belong—except in Iran, where it's law, not waning convention.

Because his milkweed tuffs of hair are so pale and have nothing to do with me. And his brutality: pinching, hitting and biting us, his face set and eyes wide to absorb reactions, then belly laughing when we cry out—an ecstatic heave so absorbing we forget pain and laugh too.

Because who my children are is celestial mystery. And every time I look at them, I experience a recognition that's primordial: They grew in my body, growing limbs, sparking cells, beating hearts, but also strangeness.

Where did you come from? How come I get to have you?

My name because it's my family's, and I can tell my father this now: I understand your drive to control. When you're in control, you have less to fear.

The act of naming is about protection as much as possession.

My children; I'm more theirs than they'll ever be mine. My name is our bridge back to each other.

Because my name means power.

Sepaz Gorezam
(I'm Grateful)

My mom is looking at something on her phone, or pretending to. She doesn't want to talk to me. It's been two months since she was released from the hospital, and my brothers and I are still asking how she's doing. It's a bother. Every time she picks up the phone, it's one of us, speaking sucrose sweet: *You doing okay, Mom?*

She doesn't want to think about how she's doing. She wants everything to go back to the way it was before.

But that's impossible. We keep calling, but she rarely answers the phone now because she knows that, when we're asking if she's okay, we're also begging her not to fuck up again. And that's impossible too.

Her exception to her phone blackout is my kids. She'll answer if she knows it's them, which means I have to text her beforehand to let her know one of them wants to talk to her. I'd done this yesterday. Would she please answer the phone if Roo called in the next few minutes?

Yes, she'd replied.

Roo had wanted to see *Incredibles 2*—the new Disney movie. She'd wanted to go when her older siblings were in school. It's meant to be a treat: just her, me, the baby, and of course her Nana.

"Can Nana come?" she'd asked.

"Why don't you call her?" I'd said, knowing it would be an opportunity to get my mother out, or at least talking to someone, even if that person was a honey-tongued three-year-old—Roo's speech so gooey thick that it's difficult to understand.

My mom understood enough of what Roo was saying to agree to come with us to the movie the next day. She'd meet us at our house, and we'd drive to the theatre together. This is what Roo told me as she handed back the phone.

"Nana didn't want to speak to me?"

Roo shook her head and laughed, bouncing down the hall, calling for her siblings; presumably so she could rub their noses in her good luck.

A few minutes later, I received a text from my mom: *Let me know the details (i.e. showtime) and I'll be at your place an hour before.*

I repressed the urge to tell her that we'd pick her up. She's fine to drive, I told myself. She's fine to drive now.

I texted my brothers to let them know I'd be seeing Mom tomorrow. *Triumph!* I'd typed.

Make sure you talk to her about how she's doing, they'd replied. *Also ask if she's been taking her medication. Ask if she has all her vitamins. Ask if she's been to see her doctor.*

———— The doctor at the hospital had told her: "This would have got much worse had your kids not pushed you to come in. You should thank them."

She looked at each of us in turn.

"Yeah right," she'd said.

———— I know I hadn't pushed her enough. I hadn't believed her. I believed she was sick. I just didn't trust the reasons she'd given me. Matthew and I were arranging our wills at our lawyer's office when my younger brother called to say that mom wasn't well. I'd been distracted.

She hadn't been able to eat in over twenty-four hours, my brother reported. My mom, who he'd included on the call too, huffed on her end of the line. She could hardly hold down water, he'd said. She had diarrhoea and a short fuse with anyone who suggested she should see a doctor. She was making this harder than it needed to be.

My first thought was that she'd been drinking again—likely a lot, and over the course of several days. The signs of a hangover were easy to recognize: the nausea, anxiety, and irritability. So I became annoyed instead of concerned. My mother knew alcohol was contraindicated with the medication she was supposed to be taking for her anxiety and depression. She knew this, and she was still killing herself, I thought.

My sympathy was running thin.

My break from booze had created in me a truncated tolerance for the antics of those who continued to drink. Call it the hypocritical plight of the converted.

As my younger brother conference-called in my older brother, I made eye contact with Matthew. He raised an eyebrow at me. I shrugged, offering a weak smile. Matthew was always being endlessly patient with me. I took a deep breath.

Your mom. She's not well. I said this to myself, and I told myself it didn't matter why. It didn't matter whether it was because she was drinking, or wasn't taking her medication, or because she had the flu, or a combination of those things. She was sick. I turned in to face the wall and lowered my voice.

She needed to get to the hospital, I'd said. We'd all said it, except my mom, who maintained that she was too sick to even leave the proximity of the bathroom. Go, my older brother had said to her, or we'll call an ambulance.

I was 45 minutes away. An ambulance could be there in 15 minutes. This is how I explained away my not wanting to drive her myself. The truth was I tired of this shit. I was afraid of what I'd say, and what she'd do if I went to her.

The truth was, I was scared.

She drove herself and was admitted a few hours later. She had a severe viral infection, and was placed in isolation. When my brothers and I visited later than night, we were told we had to wear gowns, masks, and gloves to enter her room. Her arms were bruised from the IVs and blood tests; her skin was ashen, eyes cloudy, and her feet, for some reason, were bruised too. She couldn't tell us how or why.

"Do you want us to tell Dad to come back early?" My younger brother was asking because my father was away in Iran, visiting family.

She'd been dozy, but at the mention of bringing my dad home she sat up, eyes wide. "No! Absolutely not!"

During the two nights she spent in the hospital, doctors worked to find out what was causing her elevated tropin levels. Tropin is a globular protein complex that's part of muscle contraction. When it's too high, it can be a sign of a stressed system—specifically, a stressed heart. The test results came back, but my mother said they still didn't know what was wrong.

I knew I had to speak with the doctor directly. I asked my mother's permission and she gave it, reluctantly, likely knowing that refusal would be even more suspicious than her claim that there were no answers yet.

"If you must," she said. "I've already been insulted and patronized so often. What more can you do?"

She used this anger to try to keep us, her children, at bay. I recognized the strategy. I'd used it myself, many times, to make Matthew leave me alone so I could do what I wanted in peace. Well, not in peace, exactly, but at least so I wouldn't have to look at myself.

———◆ I waited in my protective gear outside my mom's hospital room for the doctor's visit until the kids were bored and starting to be disruptive, then left a message with a nurse asking the doctor to call me.

He did, later that day, and he confirmed my suspicions. He'd already informed her that her elevated tropin levels were the result of an overburdened body. She should have gone to a doctor days ago. She was extremely dehydrated and her electrolytes were out of whack.

"Because of the flu?" I'd asked.

"Not entirely. We're also aware of the fact that there are some medications she should have been taking to treat her thyroid, depression and anxiety."

"Yes," I'd said.

"She admits she hasn't been taking them."

"Oh."

"So this is going to be making it hard for her body to work, and for her to do the things she needs to do to take care of herself. She's malnourished, for instance. It's hard to say how long she's been neglecting herself like this, but it predates this flu."

———⸱ When I was 16 years old, as part of a high school credit requirement, I'd volunteered at a nursing home in town, playing cards and doing manicures for the residents, some not much older than my mother. I was instructed by a staff member to wear latex gloves. There was literally shit under their nails. When I prepared them, filing and cleaning, I'd have to use a small, wedged bamboo stick to scrape the filth out. The residents weren't being dirty intentionally, the staff member had explained, but when people get older, they sometimes forget how to take care of themselves. Making sure the residents ate, and stayed hydrated and as clean as possible was a big part of the staff's job.

I remembered this experience while listening to the doctor, and thought of my mom sitting on her couch at home, the way I'd seen her so many times before: body slack, eyes glazed, staring at the TV surrounded by balled up Kleenexes, throat lozenge wrappers, and half-empty, half-crushed water bottles. I thought of my mother sitting like this, totally alone, and felt the air go out of my body. *Whoosh.* A world without oxygen.

"Did you want to speak with her?" The doctor was asking.

I didn't want to. I didn't want to admit that my mother was this sick and that I hadn't bothered to help her. I took a deep breath.

"Yes," I said. "I think I should."

A second later, my mother was saying: "I don't want to hear it."

"I'm not going to say anything. But please, Mom, promise you'll do whatever you have to do to get better."

"I've already heard it from the doctor. He lectured me for 30 minutes. I don't need to hear anymore."

"I know. Just saying I'll help. Whatever you need."

"I need to be left alone."

Then I heard the doctor's voice, after she'd handed the phone back. "For the record," he said, "I wouldn't say I lectured her."

"I know," I said. "This is a sensitive subject for her."

"It's a sensitive subject for most of us, but she needs to hear it." Another pause, then he laughed. "She's giving me a dirty look now."

"Yeah, you're not going to be her favourite person."

"Neither are you," he said, "if you encourage her to make the changes she needs to. Which you should. This is serious, life threatening."

My mother, in the background: "I said I'll start taking my medications! I said I'd start drinking more water and not skipping meals! I don't need help!"

I told Matt about this conversation when he got home that night. I said: "God, how did you do this with me? How did you tolerate me when you didn't believe me?"

"I always believed *in* you," he said. "I just didn't always trust you."

The next morning, I got up early to work out. I was going to go back to the hospital later on, and I needed to burn through the raw feeling: My nerves were on the outside of my skin. My phone had been ringing and buzzing all night with family chats.

What do we do about Mom?

Should we get Dad to come home anyway?

How are you, Mom?

Mom, have you got any more blood work back yet?

Mom?

The workout didn't help much. I was less tired, but still jittery. Matt was asking me questions and I couldn't form the answers. These were simple questions about whether or not I was going to be home from the hospital in time to get the kids from school, or whether I wanted a cup of coffee.

"Stop," I told him, tapping my temple. "Everything's moving too fast. There's too much going on."

"Do you want to go for a run?" He said he'd stay home an hour later from work to be with the kids so I could head out. "Just enjoy the time by yourself."

Nuala had joined me for my workout downstairs, and a few times I'd gotten frustrated with her questions. I could hardly breathe, let alone tell her why I was doing a switch lunge or whether I liked the pink yoga mat better than the purple.

"Nuala!" I'd said, panting. "Enough!"

She'd slinked away back upstairs, and I'd pushed on. Nothing felt better.

"You don't have to go," Matt said. "But if you still have the energy to burn, go for it."

It's a thin, blurry line: the one between exercise as therapy and exercise as obsession. I had to think for a moment: I had to decide which I was encouraging. Was I running because I thought I needed to look a certain way? Or was I running because I wanted to feel a certain way? It can get hard to tell, because, either way, I'd be running to make something disappear.

Nuala walked in the kitchen and stopped when she saw me. I motioned her over, kneeling down on one leg and putting my forehead to hers. "I'm sorry, okay? I shouldn't have been short with you."

She wrapped her arms around my neck. "It's all right. I know you're just worried about Nana." She fiddled with one of the straps of my sports bra. "And, I think you should go on that run."

I pulled away, looking into her face. I was already someone who was too much, someone she needed a break from. Does the weight of our mothers always go from being reassuring to suffocating? From a hand holding you up to a hand pushing you down? I didn't want to believe that I'd thought this of my mother. I pictured my mother's hands folded in her lap, thumbs, twiddling—something she said her mother did too. I pictured her hand holding mine as we moved through backlit streets of a Hong Kong night market, and I could still feel her warm, firm grasp. Nuala started to laugh, my furrowed expression of puzzled hurt amusing her.

"Mom!" She threw up her arms. "Go run!"

———+ My mom was released from the hospital when her blood tests showed signs of improvement. Rather than going home, she stayed with me for a while, against her will. My brothers and I insisted that we were worried about her and wanted her with someone who could make sure she'd be alright.

"I'm not a child," she repeated.

Do you need me to come home? My dad texted again.

"No!" My mom was adamant when we repeated his offer. "Don't let him come back yet!"

"Then you've got to stay with me," I said.

"It's because we love you," my brothers said.

She rolled her eyes. *Fine.*

She stayed with me because, my brothers said, I'd been through this sort of thing myself: a mental health crisis. I'd know what she needs. She also stayed with me because I was home during the day, writing, talking care of the kids. I could make sure she was resting, taking her meds and eating well. She did these things without any prompting from me.

"What the doctor said about my situation being life-threatening ... that scared me," she'd told me on her third morning at my house. She was looking healthier but still tired. "I couldn't sleep last night because I kept playing it over and over in my mind."

"I know, Mom." I know the fear of realizing what you're capable of doing to yourself, and when you've taken things too far, or are about to. Somewhere along the line, though, you have to decide for yourself how much your life means to you. You can decide that it's not worth it. You can decide to push on in the hope that eventually the days you spend pushing will be fewer than the days when you can just float. There's really no wrong answer, either.

"Fear isn't necessarily a bad thing," I told my mom. "Fear can be a good motivator."

She sucked in her lips and nodded her head. She looked as if she was going to cry. "Mom," I said. "It'll be all right. I promise."

———→ My mom stayed with me for a week. I would have liked her to stay longer, but it was obvious she wanted to get home, and I didn't want to make her feel trapped, or any more trapped than she already did. Before she left, I hired a local lady to clean her house so she had the peace of mind of returning to a tidy space.

No.

So I had the peace of mind of knowing that she'd be returning to in a tidy place.

No.

Both. There's seldom ever a single reason for anything.

———→ My mother, Roo, and I are on our way to the movie. The tree limbs are throwing themselves over the road and the curls of Roo's hair seem as intricate as a dragonfly's wings.

My mom is complaining about my dad making a mess of the house. She's kept on the cleaning lady, though.

"So," she says, "at least it won't be a pigsty for long."

"That's great! When is she going to come again?" I'm trying to steer her away from the topic of my father. Their complaining about each other has become more agitating to me as I've gotten older.

"Later this week."

It's more agitating because despite everything that's happened, I want them to learn to live with each other in relative harmony.

"And," my mom says, "I've asked her to bring her son, to do some work in the garden."

Gardening used to be something my mom loved. She still does, in small bits, but the gardens at her new home require more tending than she wants to give them.

"It's good that you're putting yourself first." I think back to the gardens at the house they most recently moved from, how they'd grown epic in Havisham-ian proportions; overgrown and gnarly. "Good too, that you're being realistic about what you're capable of."

My mom's silent.

"You know what I mean. It takes time to get better."

She's still silent. I rush on.

"I'm so glad you are. You're doing a great job, Ma."

And she is. I'm careful to keep my praise general, though. When I first started trying to get better, I didn't like to be reminded of how sick I was—of how far there was to go. I'd had to acknowledge the depth and breadth of my condition in all of its terrifying complexity, but if I spent any more time dwelling on it, it would drown me again. When you're broken, sometimes the best way to hold yourself together is to use momentum. You just have to move, and keep moving until it comes naturally.

In the backside of the van, Roo flexes, straining against the straps of her car seat.

"Imma gonna ... bust ... free!" She says, grunting. When I make quizzical eye contact with her in the rearview mirror, she bursts into a ribboned explosion of giggles.

"Superhero baby!" She squeaks.

I turn the conversation with my mom to something I know she'd want to talk about: my older brother's wedding. The event is a few months away.

"Have you found your dress yet?"

She looks up, confused.

"For the wedding?"

Still confused.

"Your son's?"

"Oh!" she says, putting her phone down. "Yes, yes. Well, no. I have ordered a couple and am going to see which I like best."

"Sounds like a solid plan."

"And just so you know, I haven't lost my mind."

"Huh?"

"I'm going to more than one wedding this season."

Yes. I remember that one is for the daughter of a childhood friend. She'd told me.

"I know, Mom. I wasn't thinking that you'd lost your mind." I'm not going to get drawn into a fight. It's another thing I remember about when I first started trying to get better: Sometimes, you're hurting, and you want someone else to hurt too.

"What do the dresses look like? That you ordered?"

"You know me. Dark, but not black, of course. One is dark blue with a floral print with sleeves. Women my age shouldn't show their arms."

"Says who?"

"It's just not a good look."

"Says who? If you want to show your arms, show your arms." I raise my voice. "Right, Roo? Nana should show her guns!"

Roo flexes both her arms and gives us her biggest, dimpled smile.

"I don't know." My mom shakes her head, raising one arm and grabbing the skin that hangs from the back of it. She's taking her thyroid medication regularly now, but hasn't gained back much weight. "I wouldn't feel comfortable."

"Well, if you wouldn't feel comfortable, then don't. But don't avoid wearing something you like because of what you're afraid people will think."

"You're right. I guess it comes from living with your father. He's so critical."

Another reason my parents' picking at each other bothers me more as I get older: because after a certain age, time stops flying, and starts evaporating. I don't want them to spend any more time being unhappy.

"I'm sure that whatever you pick will be wonderful."

"You know what they say: The mother of the groom just has to show up, shut up, and not wear beige." I did know they said that, but only because she'd told me before.

I want to keep the conversation buoyant. I ask: "What did your mom wear to your wedding?"

"She wasn't at my wedding. She'd died by then."

"Shit, Mom. I'm sorry." I'd known that, but had forgotten.

"It's okay," she says. "She died ten months before I was married. Your grandfather always told me how much she would have loved to have been there."

I swallow hard.

"I'm sorry, Mom. I forgot."

"Of course, it made me sad," she said. "But my saddest memory of my mother was right before she died. Did I ever tell you about this?"

I shake my head.

"My mom, dad, and I were at the cottage, and I'd fallen asleep in the middle of the afternoon on the couch in front of the fireplace. Dad was outside gardening, and Mom was upstairs in bed. She was very unwell at the time. Her leg had already been amputated, so she relied on my dad for just about everything."

"Amputated because of the diabetes?"

"Indirectly. Her leg was amputated because of gangrene."

"What?!" I'd never heard this before.

"She had gangrene from pushing the pedals on our piano. She used to sit on the bench and do it to keep her feet moving because the diabetes made them swell. The diabetes also made her lose feeling in her feet, though, so when all the pumping caused her shoe to rub against her skin and become infected, she didn't really notice."

"How do you not notice that?" As someone chronically and hypochondriacally aware of my body, I can't make sense of this information.

"Well, you know about how she hated doctors." We're at a red light, and I've turned to stare at her. My mom shrugs. "It was a different time. Different attitudes."

"Wow. I mean ... wow." I want to ask more about my grandmother's reluctance with regard to doctors, but given my mother's attitude about seeking medical help, I drop it. "Okay, so what happened?"

"Maybe it was a sense of foreboding, but when I woke up out of that nap, I was sadder than I'd ever been in my life. I remember just lying there feeling lost—absolutely lost."

I look at my hands and see my grip is white-knuckled on the steering wheel. My mom is chatting openly and easily, however, and I realize this conversation is more difficult for me than for her. She's lived with this story for years, but it's the first time I'm hearing about it. I wasn't prepared. I didn't mean to trip into this memory with her, but I can see everything: my young mother napping on the cottage's old green couch, the sun casting streamers of light through the window, the room otherwise unlit. The old clock outside the kitchen door would have been ticktocking. You'd be able to hear the electric hum of insects in the yard, too numerous to identify, but you'd ride their throbbing rise and fall, perfectly synchronized. Also, in the room: the scent of apple and old dry wood.

Mom said: "Later that day, my dad went upstairs to check on my mom and bring her something to eat. After she was diagnosed with diabetes, he made all her meals for her. He wanted to keep her healthy. She'd gotten quite big by then."

"How big?"

"Pretty big. But when my dad took charge of her diet, she lost a lot of weight. He wasn't controlling, but he followed the doctor-recom-mended diet exactly. It worked. She was never as small as she was when she was younger, but she was better."

In one picture of my grandmother in her twenties, she's so thin that her hip bones are visible ridges under her dress.

"Okay. So …?"

"When my dad was upstairs, I heard her scream. I was at the bottom of the stairs by then, on the way to the bathroom, and when I heard her, the first thing I thought was: 'What's she complaining about now?'"

"Did she complain a lot?"

"In the end, yes. Dad took very good care of her, but she didn't always make easy for him. It was embarrassing to have the windows open, because of her yelling."

"Yelling what? Why?"

"Her language was never horrible. She didn't really swear, but there was a lot of 'God damn it'—that sort of thing. As for why, I couldn't tell you now, although I'm sure I could have then. My mother wasn't well, mentally. It wasn't something people talked about then or would know how to if they did."

In the back seat, Roo is blowing spit bubbles and babbling to no one in particular.

"When my mother screamed, I realized later, it must have been because she'd had her stroke. That must have been the blood clot. We got her to the hospital, but she died shortly after."

"Oh, Mom."

"I'd thought that she was just being difficult."

"You didn't know."

She exhales. "But I shouldn't have even thought it."

I've been so fortunate; to have had the same dismissive thoughts about my mom's pain when she was sick, and still get to have her here. I reach over and squeeze her hand. It's not a perfect process, this evolu-tion of self and other, the self as other, the other as self: the crucial dissolution of divisions.

Identity Model

THE CASHIER AT the hardware store smells of synthetic strawberry and has a large birthmark running up from her chest to her neck. It looks like the North American continent turned upside down. She's wearing a bruised-purple, deep-cut V-neck, so I can see almost all of it.

"You have a very exotic look," she says. "What *are* you?"

Her fair skin is heavily freckled too, so I can't guess her age. She might be thirtyish, maybe forty? I'm even more confounded by the thick, dark brown eyebrows she's drawn over what I can only guess from her strawberry-blonde hair must be very fair brows. Her hair is chin-length, and it looks as if it's been shorn off with shears.

"Sorry?" I ask, blinking her into focus.

"Where are you from?" She leans over the counter and says this slowly, emphatically. Her lips are fat, like plump worms after rain. I lick my lips.

"I'm from here?" I sound as if I am asking her.

"No, I mean where were you born?"

It takes me a moment, but I finally get it. My exotic look.

"I was born here," I say. "Well, not here, exactly, but in Toronto."

She rolls her eyes. "You know what I mean. What's your background?"

I know what she means, but I am not going to give her what she wants, at least not right away. "My mother is sixth-generation Canadian."

Her eyes are the colour of dead grass.

"And my father," I say, pretending to root around in my purse for something, just so I can drag it out, be more difficult, "is from Iran."

"That's it! Oh, what a shame!" She doesn't look like she means this. She's pouting, her freckled lips wet, but her face is flushed, excited. Her eyes glow. "I've obviously never been"—(obviously)—"but you really can't blame people for hating your people."

"Sorry?"

"You know, because of ISIS and all."

"Because of ISIS?"

"Yes, people in that part of the world, they're ISIS, right? And so you can't blame us for hating them." She bags my batteries, and the double-sided mounting tape I've come here for. "And you're Muslim, right?"

"No. Well, no, I was raised Muslim. Kind of." I know what is happening, but I can't seem to find the words to stop it. She's just barrelling forward and I'm amazed by it all. The confidence of her trajectory is astounding.

"See? That's what I mean! Just a shame." She shakes her head, her uneven hair swinging like a scythe. I fight the sudden impulse to run and hide. She's staring at me with those eyes, and I can't stop thinking about how there's a burn ban in effect. No lighting fires.

Words eventually come and when they do, they come too quickly. "Just because someone's Iranian doesn't mean they're with ISIS." I'm blurting this out, pumping my lips because I can't feel my heart beating. Inside me, it's all very quiet. "And just because they're Muslim doesn't mean they're with ISIS. They're not the same things."

Run, I think.

"But they can be." She nods. "Hey!" She's shouting at someone behind me and waving her over. "Guess what she is? Guess where she's from?"

Hide.

The woman looks nervous, glancing back and forth between us; she appears to be thinking the same thing as me: *How did I get dragged into this?*

"Um," the woman says, "Canada?"

"No, no!" Between the two women in front of her, the cashier obviously thinks she's dealing with idiots. "What do you think she *is*? Her nationality."

"Um, Canadian?"

Now the cashier looks both annoyed and triumphant, her eyes shining, her smile, wide. Hello, Miss Universe.

"She's Muslim!"

"I'm not sure that's a nationality," the woman says.

"Can you believe it? Look at her!" Both women look me up and down. I'm suddenly aware of my neon green flip-flops, silver nail polish. My black compression tights and "This Parade is Gay" tank-top. "I mean, really! You'd never guess it!"

"I'm half-white too," I say. But she's not listening.

In the last few months, I'd read a paper on the biracial identity—one of the few academic studies I've found on the biracial psyche. I'd checked the publication date: 1996. Before then, relatively little seems to have been written on the subject. Over the course of the paper, the author outlined how research has found that the biggest challenge for biracial people is moving between the various labels and mislabels people affix to them, and their own conceptions of themselves.

I'd noticed immediately that the author didn't make a distinction between the biracial experience of men and women. Women almost always have a harder time escaping the heft of labels, making their challenge, to my mind, considerably greater. I remember scrolling back up to the top of the paper, and saw, just as I'd suspected, that the author was biracial, and a man. The oversight was still critical, but now also explainable. We often only see as far as ourselves.

I also remember that the author of the study had identified three stages in the development and resolution of the biracial, bicultural identity: The first stage was awareness of the difference and dissonance between other people's perceptions and their self-perception. This usually began between the ages of eight to ten. Next, there was the struggle for acceptance, which starts in late adolescence, and usually runs into early adulthood. The final stage is acceptance, which can take place any time between late adolescence and mature adulthood. And the author was not talking about acceptance by others. This may or may never happen. He was referring to acceptance of oneself.

I have to resist the urge to view his conclusions as pat. I can attest to the reality of these transitions: the unsettling realization of my different-ness shortly after I began school, when other kids let me know that they'd noticed I wasn't like them—but someone other. The way I looked wasn't always the giveaway. To this day, most people assume I am Italian, Portuguese, Spanish, or Greek. It's often only other Iranians who can pick me out. What usually set me apart was my name. Like the colour of your skin, your name is one of those things you don't question, until it's called into question by someone else. I learned to question my name almost as soon as I began to have to use it to introduce myself. New friends, teachers at school—all were puzzled. It's not that there weren't people with ethnic names in my schools. There were, at least in the schools I went to in the city. But their names could be linked to a distinct culture of origin. Mine confounded people. My dad, it seems, had not been absolutely confident about its spelling, so he and my mom devised a new one that would also look more familiar to Western people; it looked like a corruption of Holly. Sometimes, when I'm in what appears to be uniformly white company and I don't have the will to explain or position myself, which inevitably happens from time to time, I just say Holly is my name. I choose sides.

My name is not even recognizable to most Iranian people at first. When I tell another Iranian my name, they often have to think about it for a moment. I see them repeating it to themselves in their heads, lips mouthing it over and over until they've twisted it into its more common pronunciation. Hal-lay. Not Hal-ly. They always smile, faces brightening, as if they've solved a little riddle. Yes, yes! Of course!

Most of my relatives on my father's side call me Hallay. The majority of the relatives on my mother's side call me Holly. My husband, my brothers, my parents, and my friends: they use the hybrid.

I've never minded either version. I've come to enjoy the fluidity this trifecta of names affords me: I can pick and choose who I want to be; who I think I need to be at any given time. But at first, when I was younger, I didn't mind because I didn't care to draw more attention to myself by correcting anyone. The way I looked was already setting me apart: I was a pudgy girl with a fine, dark moustache on her upper lip, and a prominent nose. Surrounded by my lithe, 'stache-free, cutesy-schnozed female peers, I was already falling short of standards of beauty. As I said, the author of the paper doesn't make the distinction between men's biracial, bicultural experience and that of women, but there are notable differences.

As my therapist had pointed out years ago, women have to endure most of the aesthetic expectations in any culture. Add conflicting moral expectations to the equation, and it's bound to get painfully confusing. It's easier to let the less desirable parts of oneself fade into the background.

This attempt to confront and dissolve the dissonance that separates oneself from others would be the second stage of the biracial identity paradigm outlined in that paper: the struggle for acceptance. This is when biracial individuals attempt to blend in. In school, I longed to be a Victoria or Sarah or Jennifer. And not just to have such a name, but to have that unequivocal lightness of being that girls with those names seemed to exude.

Acceptance—the last stage in the biracial identity model. This is where I resisted the author's findings. Up to this point, I could bob along, nodding my head and agreeing with everything. But when I came across the word "acceptance," I felt that familiar sense of rebellion ignite in my chest. Acceptance means compliance. This, in turn, means giving up, accepting the things you cannot change, and I have never been able to do that. I've been told I have to accept my genetics: what my genetics make me, and what they don't. I've been told I have to accept my gender, and all of the ways being female would limit my life. There was nothing I could do about it. Actually, there was nothing I was *supposed* to do about it.

Nowadays, I read about the body acceptance movement, which at first seems like a good thing. After all, you're vowing to stop trying to be someone you're not. You're saying that you're going to take on your true self. Still, the project seems defeated by its very definition. Accept-ance. I accept. I accept this body—and then, the seemingly unspoken murmur: if I have to, and even though I don't like it.

Body acceptance is too depressing to tolerate. Body love—that's great. Body celebration, sure. But not acceptance—never that.

You never have to lower your standards, but you may have to ad-just them. This is something I started telling myself when I was preg-nant, and I'd get frustrated because my body wouldn't let me do some-thing I could usually do. Maybe it was tying my shoe without getting winded, or sitting upright without excruciating pain in my ribs, or staying awake past 8 p.m. Whatever the obstacle, I'd remind myself to refocus. The standards I was setting weren't unattainable because I wasn't enough. They were unattainable because *they* weren't enough. They weren't enough to encapsulate who I was that day, that month, or even that minute. You're allowed to be who you need to be to get by. You're allowed to change. But this isn't the same as accepting your lot in life. This isn't settling.

This is why the author's mention of acceptance made me recoil. I've lived the transitions he describes, and while I can see where each moment—each stab at self-awareness and acceptance—may align with this paradigm, my life doesn't feel this tidy. Given my compulsion for cleanliness, you'd think I'd crave his compact explanation, that I'd eat it up. I'm surprised myself. This used to be enough. When I was a child and was first registering my need to keep my life ordered, I would lit-erally sweep dirt under the rug and try to pretend it didn't exist. As a long-term solution, it didn't work. There'd be relief for a bit; the floor would stare back with its unblemished white, but then it would get dirty again. There's only so much room under a rug. The disaster I would finally have to deal with was far worse than the initial mess. It's a lesson that seems obvious now. It's even more obvious in light of how my tendency to try to short-cut my pain was repeated later in life, when I used alcohol and pills to mask the mess.

To the author's credit, though, he never claimed that the process of coming to terms with oneself would be tidy. His neat summation of his research was an artifact of the convention of academic writing, more than a denial of the muddled nature of the experience. He readily allowed that the final stage, acceptance, is an ongoing process—a process we can more easily arrive at, over and over again if necessary, only after going through the first two stages.

Despite how much I want to distance myself from the term, acceptance is at the pummelled, still-beating heart of this final stage. I will have to continually accept who I am. And no matter how much I think I know exactly who I am, the world will continue to break me down, and force me to choose again.

I am forced to choose almost every day.

Which one am I?

Choose.

——— Two years ago, some asshole got trigger-happy in a mosque in Quebec City, and Nuala, who was watching the news, was inconsolable. She was falling apart, her sobs shaking her hair loose from its ponytail. I was next, she was sure of it. She was next. Everyone she loved was going to die. But she had to be at school in thirty minutes, and I had a full day of meetings and deadlines. There was cereal all over the floor, and I needed to fit in a workout before I could do anything, and everything was happening too fast.

I had to choose. Nuala was just five years old, and this was before my encounter with the woman at the hardware store. Still, it was the first time I wanted to totally deny one half of me. Nuala was crying so hard that I couldn't catch the words tripping out of her mouth. Her speech was fumbled, frantic.

"I don't speak Farsi, right? You don't speak Farsi? Don't speak Farsi! Gramps can't speak Farsi, right?"

I was still struggling to understand how she had made the connection between the language and the shooting.

She jabbed a finger in the direction of the television. Her finger, her hands: they still had a toddler's chubby-knuckled fullness. I turned to the TV. The man being interviewed was speaking Farsi, a language she didn't understand but had come to recognize. I thought, okay, this I can handle. This, I can deflect.

"Honey, Farsi is a language," I explained. "And those people didn't get shot because they were speaking Farsi."

"Then why?"

"Because they were Muslim, and that man doesn't like the Muslim religion."

"Why?"

"Because he's not a very nice person."

She gulped, swallowing spit, snot. My explanation, she considered it.

"Am I Muslim?"

"No."

"Are you? Is Gramps?" Her tears plastered wisps of duckling hair to her forehead, cheeks, and neck. Her finger was still pointing at the TV, unmoving. *Choose.*

"Honey, don't worry about us." I brushed her hair back and picked the heavy mass of white-blonde, dark-blonde, and blonde-blonde off her shoulders to help cool her down. Her name, Irish and picked out before her birth, means fair shoulders. It is by all accounts well suited to her. Except in the summer, when her skin deepens to an unfathomably rapt golden brown. It's unfathomable if you don't know her background.

"Are you Muslim?" Nuala repeats, her voice gaining urgency. I can feel my heart pushing up my throat. Calm down.

"Honey, you don't have to …"

"Don't be, Mommy. Please promise!" Her blue eyes are backlit, wide, like she's been plugged into the surging pulse of the universe: uncertain, uncontrollable, incomprehensible.

"Mommy," she said, "*promise* you won't be anything at all."

"Okay," I promised, pulling her head to my chest and stroking her hair. "Shush, now. Okay."

I'm nothing.

This feels safer. But I also know that being nothing is only easy in theory. The *practice* of actually being no one though, that's tough. It

takes effort to disappear. The effort I made to disassociate from myself
—even a part of myself—has shown me that I'm way more invested in
the idea of myself as a whole than I thought. Chip away as I try, deny
as I may, but I keep trying to pull myself back together.

The author of the study offered a more clinical explanation, saying
that the biracial and bicultural person perpetually strives for a sense of
being whole. Throughout their lives, a biracial and bicultural person
will learn to preserve this identity of being both things, and neither
thing, through that agile and hard-earned acceptance of self.

Again, much of what the author says sounds true, but it also makes
me feel like I'm being shown a blueprint of the house I've lived in my
whole life: familiar but impersonal. While I admire the research and
have great respect for his attempt to shed light on the complexities of
the biracial experience, I'm also inclined to keep the findings at arm's
length. I've already admitted that the narrow parameters of the study
are not completely the author's fault. The systematic containment of his
research is an aspect of the nature of the academic medium in which
he presents his work. My response is also a natural result, which, as the
paper suggests, took years of learning from dissonance and struggle to
acquire. You're born, and you're force-fed these labels. Labels can be
hard to swallow at the best of times, and when no label quite fits you—
when you spill out of nomenclature—they can make you gag. Still, the
choice is yours. You can keep swallowing them, bursting with mean-
inglessness and condemned to endless hunger; or you can eventually
begin to notice that you don't always have to make a choice, since your
choice often won't matter anyway: people are going to see in you whatever way they want to see, and you have little to no control over that.

When I left that hardware store that day, I called my mom to tell
her what had happened. I told her about how the woman had another
woman guessing my race.

"She completely overlooked the fact I was also half-white, and
really just kept going on about my being Iranian, or Muslim, because
to her mind, they were the same thing."

"That's odd," she'd said. "I never think of you as biracial. Bicultural,
maybe, but not biracial."

I think back again to what that therapist had told me: about how being biracial doesn't necessarily set you up for the same challenges as being both biracial and bicultural. You can be of two different races, but have similar cultural backgrounds, and never encounter much friction as a result of your biracial identity.

"In my case," I say, "it's the same thing. But you're missing the point, Mom. She was just so painfully ignorant."

But what bothered me most, I realized, was not that she was ignorant. I had long been fully aware that ignorant people existed. What bothered me was that I hadn't set her straight. I could argue it was because I'd been too stunned, and there was an element of that, but I'd also reverted to my adolescent self. I'd wanted to erase the parts of myself that were turning me into a spectacle.

I should have been more forceful. Things need to change.

Despite body-positive movements, mental health awareness campaigns, an increase in racial and cultural sensitivity, and the proliferation of disturbing studies that show substance abuse among women is on the rise, many people still aren't giving these problems and intersections the attention they deserve. And many of the women who are suffering are themselves among those not engaging. This, I think, is the biggest problem of all, especially since there are more biracial and multicultural people than ever, and given that our digital tether means that we are more doggedly being pursued by images of perfection—be it of the physical or the mental kind. Everywhere I turn, there's another meme telling me how I should live my life, another social media role model sharing her transformative journey, and encouraging me to be better, stronger, faster, more beautiful, more authentic. This inspiration-saturation of other identities can get the best of people—even those who aren't struggling with their own, let alone those of us who are. It's so easy to lose yourself, to judge yourself harshly as less than—half. Less than half.

"It's tough for me to wrap my head around," my mother says. "When I look at you, I don't see your race or culture. I see you, my daughter."

People are going to see who they want to see, or are accustomed to seeing. I can try to conform myself to their expectations, or try to bend their views to mine, but after a certain point, I've got to admit: The decision to continue to suffer over a fixed identity is a choice. I see myself as one. I see myself as both. Most often, I see myself as neither. There's no doubt that in the current social climate, biracial and multiracial people are up against many challenges. But we also have a unique advantage: We are offered the chance to glimpse identity without borders. We are afforded the chance to experience humanity as it should be: undivided.

Acknowledgements

TYPICAL OF ME, I'd like to give a rambling and heartfelt thank you to the people who have directly or indirectly supported me through the writing of this book. My family—all of you: my mother and father, Matthew, Joseph, Fionnuala, Soroor, Harvey, Kevan, Kris, Rachel and Mona. Thanks also to Liam, Lucas and Aiden—just because.

Thank you to Carol and John Samis for all their support, always.

Thank you to Dr. Elizabeth Greene and Dr. George Logan. If I had never taken your classes and never received your encouragement, I don't know if I would ever have had the guts to make a go of this writing thing. To Erin Foley, my ride-or-die reader and best of friends. Thank you also to Diane Schoemperlen and Mary-Ellen Csamer, who have been ferocious believers in this project.

Continuing with the K-town connection, I'm grateful to John and Sam at iSTORM for believing in me many moons ago.

Thanks go to Stephanie Sinclair, whose interest in the project helped me take it more seriously, and Janice Zawerbny, for helping shape the earlier incarnation of this beast. To my Guernica editor, Gary Clairman, your insight and understanding has been an affirmation of all things good. Thank you for asking all the right questions. To Dr. Olga Stein, an outpouring of gratitude for your keen eye and wisdom.

Big hugs to the readers who courageously took on this book during its many gnarly stages: Kimberley Alcock, Shoilee Khan, Nila Gupta, Tiffany Short, Brittany George, and my MFA Creative Non-Fiction class, who saw *Fuse* in its sapling form. Thank you Janice Kulyk Keefer for leading such a life-changing course.

I'd also like to extend my gratitude to Dr. Stephen Shapero and Dr. Shayla Garland. I hope you both know how you've helped me.

The cover owes its inspiration to the work of Persian artist Ziba Safavian, and its current design to the extraordinary vision—and patience—of David Moratto. Thank you to Michael Mirolla and everyone at Guernica.

Thank you to George Kitahara Kich for granting me access to his paper, *The developmental process of asserting a biracial, bicultural identity.*

Finally, thank you to the Ontario Arts Council for their generous support of this project.

About the Author

HOLLAY GHADERY IS a writer living in small-town Ontario. Her fiction, non-fiction, and poetry have been published in various literary journals, including *The Malahat Review, Room, Grain*, and *The Fiddlehead*. In 2004, she graduated from Queen's University with her BAH in English Literature, and in 2007, she graduated from the University of Guelph with her Masters of Fine Arts in Creative Writing. She is the recipient of the Constance Rooke Scholarship in Creative Writing, as well as Ontario Arts Council grants for her poetry and non-fiction. You can learn more about Hollay at www.riverstreetwriting.com.

This book is made of paper from well-managed FSC® - certified forests, recycled materials, and other controlled sources.